PROVERBS

BY
RICHARD WISLOCKY

TRILOGY
A WHOLLY OWNED SUBSIDIARY OF **TBN**

Trilogy Christian Publishers
A Wholly Owned Subsidiary of Trinity Broadcasting Network
2442 Michelle Drive
Tustin, CA 92780
Copyright © 2024 by Richard Wislocky

All Scripture quotations, unless otherwise noted, taken from The Holy Bible, New International Version®, NIV® Copyright © 1973, 1978, 1984, 2011 by Biblica, Inc.® Used by permission. All rights reserved worldwide. Scripture quotations marked (KJV) taken from The Holy Bible, King James Version. Cambridge Edition: 1769.

All rights reserved, including the right to reproduce this book or portions thereof in any form whatsoever.
For information, address Trilogy Christian Publishing
Rights Department, 2442 Michelle Drive, Tustin, Ca 92780.
Trilogy Christian Publishing/ TBN and colophon are trademarks of Trinity Broadcasting Network.
For information about special discounts for bulk purchases, please contact Trilogy Christian Publishing.
Trilogy Disclaimer: The views and content expressed in this book are those of the author and may not necessarily reflect the views and doctrine of Trilogy Christian Publishing or the Trinity Broadcasting Network.

10 9 8 7 6 5 4 3 2 1
Library of Congress Cataloging-in-Publication Data is available.
ISBN 979-8-89333-163-9

ISBN 979-8-89333-164-6 (ebook)

Dedication

A great thanks to God, Jesus, the Holy Ghost, and all the warm-hearted whispers from everyone who helped write this book along the way. All glory goes to God. Amen. Amen. Amen.

Introduction

Richard Wislocky was raised and baptized Presbyterian from the time of his childhood. In his later years, he now attends two different churches and has bounced around, going to a variety of different types of churches and spiritual gatherings to get a feel for it all. His love has no limits, and through this book, you will learn the proper way to make GOoD love. It is a great spiritual guide for the modern-day man. Richard has had an extensive battle with drugs over the years and is not claiming to be perfect by any bounds. We are all still sinners in the eyes of the Lord. He's been to heaven and hell and back and has gained extensive knowledge and perspective of the spiritual realms that exist. He is also a mega-producer of various arts of all sorts, having no limits to his artistic reach and ability. For him it's about turning a non-believer into a believer with raw and absolute truths. He feels this book will help make a great connection and fill in the missing pieces to your own spiritual jigsaw puzzle. Believer or not, there is something here for everybody and all who dare to read this book. Take your time with it. Soak it in one gem after another. Read it with your spiritual eyes and behold the deeper meanings within the random but not so random words and delivery. Richard promises you that you will come out enriched with some sort of serious wisdom, and you will possess the basic foundations for the principles of GOoD love. Richard wants us to just bring love in all that we do. Live and let love. Blessings from above. No more suffering on earth. Rejoice and be glad in it. Everything is one. Energy is everything. God is everything. Amen. Amen. Amen.

"In the trinity, the Father is the manager, the Son is the lover of operations, and the Holy Spirit is the worker. He is Papa; He is Healer; He is Helper" (words of a mentally challenged child).

Every leaf on a tree is different.

The more you pray, the more you'll hear.

The dawn has a spirit.

There is still much to see, even when your eyes are shut.

When you make your father happy, you will make your Father in heaven happy too.

Jesus in the wind.

Jesus in the cloud.

Rejoice and be glad in it.

Always look at the best-case scenario.

Pray harder.

Nothing bad will ever happen to you when you're reading scripture.

Scripture is the earth's best form of medicine.

You can never have enough prayer.

Breathe in love with every breath you take, then exhale love.

It is an important skill to be able to listen.

Only a fool denies the truth when the truth is right in front of his face.

Fear of the Lord is healthy.

Fools talk endlessly and get nowhere.

You cannot force religion; it must be chosen.

A fool will always try to bring another person down into his foolery.

You can't reason or rationalize with a demon; its core is in madness.

A fool will never know when to be quiet.

A habitual sinner will always try to get you to sin with him.

Try and pick up litter at all costs. If everyone picked up one piece of trash, we'd have no litter to pick up.

Give thanks to Mother Earth regularly; it's important for the soul.

A fool repeats the same mistake.

When looking for the right answer, return to nature, and you shall find it there.

A wise man can tell the difference between right and wrong.

Trust your instincts; if it feels bad, it is.

Dream with the Lord, not against Him.

Your education should never stop; there is much to learn.

Find the common ground, and strive for peace.

Just say no to drugs.

Think with your heart and not with your groin.

Try and stay in a constant state of surrender.

Going through changes takes extreme patience.

"Do what you know to be right" (Native American commandment).

Forgiveness is key.

There is no such thing as doing bad to do good, or a south heal.

If you get smite on one cheek, then turn the other cheek.

There is much to learn from a convict; listen to what he says.

It is important to have some privacy.

Prayer is our great connector. Try to stay constant in prayer all the time.

Try and suppress your desires; they can lead you to your demise.

Never talk ill about anyone or have a tongue that tends to gossip.

Always pray for mercy no matter what.

It takes a fool to make a wise man.

A fool is usually in a satanic trap.

If you are guilty, you will pay.

Demons pray upon your guilt, and it is what usually gives them contracts to mess with you.

There is nothing more dangerous than a lack of faith.

Never take the easy way out.

When Jesus says "thrust," trust!

The devil is angry because he can't create; he can only be perverse.

Most tattoos are not a sign of God.

Being tempted by a harlot can lead to the selling of your soul.

In heaven, they record everything you do on earth, so watch what you say and do.

To become a king is an honor bestowed upon one by God.

Prepare to bring water to the desert.

Hell can find you if you're living for it.

You can't love a demon.

Pray for your enemies.

God does not like it when one holds loose sexual practices.

Never fart while you're praying.

When faith is on the line, patience must be the line.

Be careful about what you look for because you just might find it.

Stay clear of greedy men.

Don't talk babble if you do not know the answer.

Usually, the less said, the better.

Be friends with both the rich and the poor.

Proverbs

Give your children what you wish your dad would have given you.

There is always some truth in both sides of the story.

The common ground is to achieve equality.

The purpose of chess is to stalemate your opponent.

Be slow to judgment; always listen for all the details.

It's the little things that matter and make things special.

You have to have hope when you have no hope.

Your faith is how far you're willing to take it.

To build faith, you need to take a risk from time to time.

There are two steps before a leap of faith.

Without a good balance of things, you are useless.

Excess will most likely lead to failure, which can then lead to success, but that's a really rough road.

Lustful ways usually begin with eager eyes.

You are what you see.

Everything you know is a part of you; it's only a matter of which part and how much of you is being shown.

You don't need heat that will cause uncertainty and doubt.

In a crisis situation, it is important to stay in prayer.

Without prayer, we are spiritually dead.

If you have to ask, then it usually is.

Be the love you wish you had when dealing with others.

It is important to give back and be grateful.

Silence is a weapon for the brave.

The secret of success is to cop a flow at least once a day in some fashion; then, you will die a successful man.

Hitting the flow on the dance floor is important for spiritual growth.

It is an honor to give praise to God for even the smallest of details.

Nothing is impossible without God's love.

It is a blessing to have your sins covered; you should thank the Lord for His everlasting mercy.

Never be too big to say you're sorry.

Forgiveness is the key to the universe.

It is important to keep your body and temple healthy and fit.

Your dreams are the key to understanding your soul.

Morning prayer is crucial for a productive and blessed day.

Always do your best and give it your all.

Eagle is full effort; full effort is full victory.

Coming up short sometimes makes the success even sweeter when it's finally achieved.

There are ten failures to every great success.

A wise student always does what the teacher tells him to do.

It is important to question authority; it is how we keep them in check.

Give a meal to a hungry man.

Give a call to the ones you haven't spoken to in a while; God connects.

God connects; the devil separates.

Timing is important; be cautious and know when it's your turn to speak.

Seize the moments with your family and loved ones.

Aliens do exist; God has a plan for everything.

If you could baptize the devil, would you do it?

Jesus loves you.

Spend as little time as possible on your cell phone.

Make sure you at least plant one good seed a day.

Ask, and you shall receive.

If you associate with thieves, you probably are one.

If you're ever in an uncomfortable situation and being pressured to do something below your morals, there is always a door to exit; it's just that simple.

There is good advice to get from everyone everywhere before making a quick conclusion.

Do not play music everywhere you go. It's important to have silence as well.

Go ahead and take a leap of faith; you have everything to gain and nothing to lose.

Talk to Jesus if you want Him to talk to you. Nobody's going to talk to someone who isn't talking to him.

You should put God first in all actions you do, no matter the size.

Try and make an extra effort when fasting if you can; you will be rewarded for your extra efforts.

If you can't get out of bed, life will pass you by, and you will become poor.

If you want everlasting life, you should give all your positions away and follow Christ.

A drunkard will always be losing his money fast.

It is important not to have excess embody any aspect of your life.

Anyone can start, but it's how you finish that counts.

Always find a way to love the unlovable.

When you can't give anymore, give more.

A poor man will always give you the shirt off his back; that can't be said for the rich man.

In order to survive, you must know when to say no and stick to it; it is a skill that must be learned.

Your repentance can be heard by God and the devil because you are using your mouth to confess your sins.

When someone is paranoid, you must keep being the voice of reason, even when there is none.

Never lie to get drugs; then, it owns your soul. Don't do drugs in the first place.

If there was an eleventh commandment, it would be, "Thou shalt not do drugs."

It is important to rebuke a nightmare right away, or else it will spiritually drain you for the entire day; that's its purpose: to take you away from anything good-natured and ruin your connection to God.

Friends make the worst enemies.

In order to plant seeds, you must first go to get them. Look, and you shall find.

Pay no attention to the haters; they will reap what they sow.

Always look on the bright side of things; even if the thing is pure evil, some good can be achieved somehow. It's all about perspective.

Always try to give a little extra in your offerings.

You get what you give, so make the effort.

Do not boast about your good deeds; God sees you and knows how to reward you for your efforts.

God works on His time, so you must be patient and have faith that it will work out.

God tests your character all the time. Will you pass the tests?

Pray to God to dream together.

Don't stop praying; have an open connection twenty-four hours a day if you can. It will stop you from doing foolish activities and bring you closer to God's love.

If God punishes you, it is like what a father would do when he punishes a son. You may not like it, but it is necessary for spiritual growth and correction.

In order for God to punish you, you must have really messed up big time because His mercy is so great it takes a lot to get Him mad. He is a God of second chances, so don't keep repeating your trespasses.

God is a merciful god who has your best interests and only wants to see you thrive in success.

It is impossible to speculate what God's motives are, for His reasoning is beyond our comprehension.

The only thing you should fear in this world is losing God's love.

There are many voices one can hear, but it's the still one that comes with reason and love.

One should get baptized in adulthood so that he has a rational understanding of its importance.

Some churches can manifest demons during services, and some don't at all. God loves them all equally, and they are all important to Him.

Your salvation must be maintained like a well-executed plan that needs constant attention.

Trust your instincts; that's why God gave them to you.

Be thankful in all that you do, even for the mishaps.

Fighting with relatives and holding grudges is like killing your soul.

Always honor thy father and mother.

God made aliens too; everything has a purpose and reason.

Always try to manifest your dreams in real life. It is a powerful tool if you can achieve this merger of worlds in some fashion.

It is possible for you to see the future; if this happens, you must thank God for the opportunity and great vision.

Everything has a reason in life; do what God wants for you and try to do that to the best of your capabilities.

There is nothing like a lightning storm full of crashing thunder to remind you who's boss.

Going to war is sometimes needed but should be avoidable at all costs.

Go climb a mountain; there is much to learn.

Speak only what you know to be true; you can't base things on speculations.

Never be too embarrassed to say you're sorry, especially when it's needed.

Always lend a helping hand even if it inconveniences you.

Never make love to a woman thinking of some other woman.

Porn has the ability to rotten relationships with normal people because you will always be thinking about people in a sexual manner. It's best to keep sex off the brain and out of your mental cycles to begin with.

God favors those who can find a happy marriage.

"Till death do us part" should trump cheating behaviors and departure.

Never hit a gift horse in the mouth.

Remember always to say please and thank you.

It's only natural to have an ill thought; just rebuke it quickly, and don't let it fester.

In spiritual warfare, one must be able to mentally multitask.

Stop crossing lines that lead to destruction.

Do not covet thy neighbor's wife or goods.

A true friend is worth more than all the gold in the world.

When everything is taken from you, you still must have hope; you must keep it alive at all costs.

You cannot trust a man who tells even the littlest of a white lie.

If you want to play a fool, invite a thief over your house.

Some people can't stop lying; don't get mad at them; they can't help themselves. Pray for them.

Cheaters always finish last.

Don't forget to include the animals in your daily prayers.

Knowing the right word for the right occasion is like a fine wine.

God wants you to be sober-minded.

When the chips are down, you must always keep heart and remember you were made from love, and Jesus loves you very much.

There is no such thing as a south heal; you can never do wrong to make a right; there is only doing right to make a right.

Guns were built for one thing only: to kill.

Giving a gift is a sign of affection.

Writing your name on a wall a thousand times is vain.

Love someone when they're at their worst.

Be a rock so that God can build on.

Always help the elderly and pay close attention to what they say; there's usually wisdom to be found.

All the little things matter; try to do them for your lover.

Never open your relationship with other partners; that's not love.

Reading books is healthy for the mind.

Remember to wish your mother a happy birthday on your birthday; it's just as much hers as it is yours.

A simple hug can be so healing; try to give more hugs.

Masturbating can be an evil act.

Never pay for sex; this is a love crime.

Go with your first instinct; you're usually right.

Never judge a book by its cover, but always judge a record by one.

Never play love games; it always leads to someone getting hurt.

The person playing matchmaker usually is in love with the person whom he or she is matching.

The quiet ones are usually the wildest.

If the bad outweighs the good, it's time to go.

The number 666 finds those who are up to no good. Take it as a warning if you see this number.

Never trust a dealer with gold rings.

Gambling is a sick disease that can rob you of your freedoms and make you a spiritual slave.

Boycott the spirit of hate at all costs.

God can heal you in a second; this is why you need His love every day.

All things are possible with the love of the Lord.

When you live on the edge, you will die by the edge.

You must have love when all love can't be found.

Most people will leave you high and dry when situations get serious. This is the sad truth.

Never leave a brother in harm's way.

People who drive fast are lawbreakers.

Try and bring maximum joy wherever you go. Leave a person happier than when you came.

The gang mentality is who's the craziest one, and crazy is a demon.

Tell your parents you love them often.

Prayer saves lives.

Always try and take less than what you need.

DJs have the power to control the mood and the spirit; you must be careful who and what type of music you listen to, not all electronic music is made with a positive or friendly intention.

Some hallucinations are made by the devil to keep you in a state of temptation. He's very good at keeping you subdued.

Santa is an idol used by the devil to take away the importance of Jesus Christ on His special day.

Halloween is rooted in evil and should not be celebrated.

Anything you give power to can be used as an idol if you're not careful.

A good campfire is a good medicine.

If you're a victim of cartoon monsters, you're usually spiritually in trouble, and you must change your ways with quickness, or you will get stuck in this psychotic satanic realm.

Have no fear but fear of the Lord.

A drunkard will always go broke.

Do what you would want people to do to you.

Alcoholics usually have the demon of anger.

Sometimes, we all need a Jesus Band-Aid.

Angels assigned to you hear and see your all, so choose your words carefully; everything you do is being recorded in heaven.

Be sure to thank your guardian angel once in a while. Without him, you're burnt toast.

Try and find wise men to surround yourself with and try to learn their wisdom. And braid your tongue so that you can hear it when you find it.

Try to help those who are surrounded by the spirit of failure. Producing one victory for them in even the smallest of ways could change someone's future for the greater good.

Rush to the fire, but make sure you can put it out without being in harm's way.

Close your eyes when you kiss a woman; it means more.

A fool will repeat the same task that he knows he can't win.

A fool falls in love too quickly.

Ask permission from the higher authorities when attempting

something spiritually risky.

May your good deeds outweigh your sins.

Pray that God covers your sins; without them being covered, you're a dead man living with the shame of your mistakes for all to pass judgment on out in the open like a festering wound. And who wants that?

The devil is the greatest liar in history; be careful whom you trust psychically.

It's hard to put your trust into faceless and nameless spirits, and the lines between the truth and the lies get twisted really quickly. Sometimes, silence is golden if you can achieve that state of mind in the state you're in. This is where our faith is tested.

Be cautious; the mimics are everywhere, plotting your demise.

Recall any lost dream or vision by hitting the visionary recall button in your psyche. Try it. Recall, recall, recall. Then focus as the dream comes back to you in small flashes. Recall, recall, recall.

If you start saying and thinking evil things randomly, you are most likely under demonic attack. Try not to become a puppet. If they aren't your thoughts, you must be cautious and pray hard for God's love to conquer all these things and lift you from this demonic attack.

The devil loves to keep you high; for them, it's an easy in for them to mess with your mind. Only God can save you from his wicked schemes, and being sober helps too.

Love the Lord your Father God in heaven with all your mind, body, and soul.

It's costly to take spiritual risks; sometimes, it's necessary, but the safe road is usually a better choice. Avoid the madness.

Sing songs of praise frequently.

Do not get stuck in one thought pattern or bad action. Rebuke it, then bury it in a casket and nail it shut. Throw it in an empty grave. Then fill the grave with dirt until it's covered, and then put a gravestone above it with no name. With no name, it shall not be remembered. Then move on with your life and act like nothing ever happened. Ditch all negativity and ill thought with quickness in the rebuking graveyard. The quicker you leave it buried, the quicker you'll forget about it.

Sometimes, you can sing a song when you're in trouble to lighten the burden, but don't get trapped with it on a loop; that could sometimes be dangerous. Prepare and practice escape routes from mental loops they get stuck on cycle.

When in a spiritual bind, the TV and radio will only add to your madness in the state that you're in. Silence isn't the best answer, either. Try something creative, like writing a poem or painting a picture. Anything that keeps you in a state of positive progress is good so that you can have something psychical to show for your suffering and ill state of mind that you're in. If you have something psychical you can then later return to it, then go back into it and rework it to make it better by healing it. Art is healing in times of spiritual arrest and can help manifest some positive spiritual energy for your favor. Art can also be a great form of meditative release. The act of creation is so powerful. It changes your world in times of need.

It is tiresome to always watch over your back when you're in an altered state of mind. This also leads to paranoia. Do the right thing from the jump and get a good night's sleep and forget about being down for the game. The game is just a game and can't wait forever for your return, and it will not miss you anyway.

Knowing when to say when is a skill.

People will usually reject what they can't understand.

Fear is like cancer.

Sins lead to an early death.

Pets are important; they teach us a certain type of love that is needed for evolution.

Just surrender to love.

How can we have courage without fear?

When you have super faith, you will be tested by the devil. So be on the lookout. The closer you get to God, the more he'll try to take you out.

The devil's only purpose is to destroy and kill; there is no love in worshiping him; there is only a life of slavery.

Beware of the spiritual blinders, for they blind you from reality.

If you're in bondage in this life, you will be in bondage in the afterlife.

Good love is fulfilling like a holiday meal.

Invite strangers into your house on special occasions of celebration; all must be welcome to the joy of good company and good food.

Say your goodbyes with a "God bless you."

Sing a song of praise to the Lord.

Be thankful when someone corrects you, and be not bitter with him.

There is a lot to learn from picking up the trash of others.

There is a time to talk and a time to listen.

Never date a brother's ex-girlfriend.

One must be careful not to sell one's soul for fame or riches; there is always a price to pay in the end.

The devil has nine million ways to get you; I suggest you learn all nine million ways to avoid his scornful traps.

Too much TV can rot your soul; don't watch satanic shows that have the spirit of murder.

Watching a television show with a gun in it is usually promoting the spirit of murder and not healthy.

Beware of friend circles that are based upon fashion and fortune. There is way too much vanity.

Always be willing to take a bullet for the person you're with, no matter who they are or how much you like them.

God can open doors for you, but what good is it if you keep on shutting them?

"Be the change you want to see in the world" (Gandhi).

Shyness is nice for a good love relationship.

Good things come to those who wait.

Don't say "I love you" if you can't back it up in action.

Try not to be attracted or be seduced by women who say that they're witches, even if they're smoking hot.

One must use and have maturity when using skeletons in their art. Skeletons can quickly manifest in an evil way quickly if you're not careful.

There are mosh pits in hell.

In hell, there is a place called Santa Land.

The daily drug user should be called a freedom fighter.

How many times must you lose before you desire to win?

The way of the transgressor is hard but can lead to enlightenment in the long run. That is, if you can last through all the trials and tribulations that arise around every corner you turn.

Thank God for every breath you take; each one is a special gift.

When you're on drugs, it makes it easy for the devil to use you like a puppet to do his work; you must always be headstrong and learn to avoid the red flags if you're going to be living in this state of mind. Always be cautious of your actions and their ramifications.

A woman is like a fragile rose that sheds its peddles; even the toughest of women can break easily if she's not loved the proper way.

When you've got no more love to give, you must give more love.

Heroes are made through trials of crisis; only a few can stand up and behold this honor.

The spirit of jail is one of the darkest evil spirits to have working against you. I wish this upon no one, and to watch all these jail shows on TV only supports its growth and manifestation.

People should not glamorize serial killers and present shows about them. Their evil spirit is so strong that it can have the power to possess you even through the TV screen. TV is where Satan plants his seeds.

"Thou shalt not kill" (Exodus 20:13). This is one of the Ten Commandments.

Just because something sexual is pleasing in a dream does not mean that it's all right. The devil has many tricks. Learn to recognize what is love and what is lust.

A chronic luster has emotional problems getting attached to women. His eyes are always hungry for some other fool and plotting a filthy sexual deed.

Give your best or last bite of food to your friend as a sign of affection. Don't be selfish.

Respect is earned and given only when deserved.

Always shake a man's hand; if not, you are insulting his character.

Opposites attract and can be exciting, but in the end, it's similar styles that end up lasting longer in relationships.

The hater will stop at nothing to chew you down; most of the time, it's just extreme jealousy.

When someone is on the come up, don't be a cog in their machine. Let the good shine if it can be sustained. Love and support the effort, even if it is brief. There's more to gain through positive reinforcement than chopping someone's tree down.

Help plant trees to rebuild what we have destroyed. Mother Earth is crying.

What would you rather have, ten pennies or one dime?

Ask the questions everyone is afraid to ask but wants to.

It is wise to know when you're being tested.

Divorce should be illegal. If you have God on your side, you can always work your problems out.

Love is so simple, just love. How deep does yours go?

When the time comes to fight for what's right, will you step up? Most fail this test and keep their mouths shut to avoid conflict.

Don't ever laugh along to an evil story; you're only killing your soul.

You can't believe everything you hear; if you do, you will be confused and lost.

Sometimes, you must live for freedom and let it fly, but always stay within reason.

Love in God is true freedom.

Most of the time, you must endure strange discomfort before success. Don't quit on what you know to be right.

Give all the glory to God.

Even at a young age, you could tell good from bad; it's instinctual.

Don't continue a conversation if all you hear is foolishness.

You can teach an old dog new tricks.

No one trusts a junkie.

If you play with fire, you're going to get burned.

Where there's smoke, there's fire.

Love and show respect to everyone equally, no matter what they look like or act like.

A cool cup of water is more healing than you think. Try and drink more and always offer it to your guests.

Be grounded in love and never get uprooted.

A happy smile can go a long way in a room of changing moods.

There is nothing better than praying on your knees.

Demons like to live in filth, so keep a clean ship.

Your tongue should be the only weapon you carry.

Crying is the soul dancing and one of the greatest blessings from God.

Learn to recognize a circle spell when you see it. Demons put it on you. You can tell if you're in one because you will be going around the room looking for things and then constantly getting distracted and getting nothing done but walking in circles like a puppet.

Don't be a demon puppet; keep a sober mind.

The spirit police are a collection of guardian angels and friendly spirits who only have your best interest at heart. They may reprimand you when you get out of line, but a wise man will embrace their correction. They hold a tremendous love for your well-being. Without them, you would be screwed by the powers of the dark side, and nobody wants that horror show.

Egyptian culture uses dark magic, and it's not looked favorably upon by God. Try not to be seduced by this dark magic and mysticism. It's false power and shouldn't be tampered with; it will only bring you problems in the afterlife.

Egyptian is a slave culture; there's nothing special or loving about becoming a slave.

Casinos are slave culture; there's nothing to win but shackles and spiritual poverty.

A greedy man will cheat you.

A hooker is only looking to rob you; there is no love on her agenda.

There is something called a spiritual jacket; it holds every sin you ever made in it, and if you're lucky, someone will read them to you so that you end up repenting.

Sloths are the cutest creatures on earth, but it's an insult to be called one.

It's okay to experience sadness; just don't get drowned in the emotion. Try not to sulk for too long.

It should be a goal of yours to manifest joy in a large quantity.

Dispose of your trash in the proper receptacles; stop littering.

Sometimes, your best isn't good enough, but at least you can say you gave it your all.

"You got to know when to hold and know when to fold" (Kenny Rogers).

Never boast about yourself. A compliment should always come from somebody else and never your own tongue.

The pursuit of happiness is usually our main objective. Do what feels good and try to sustain that feeling for as long as possible.

If you can't hit the flow, don't try to force it.

Jesus is alive and well and still saving the human race on a daily basis; it's almost impossible to imagine the size of His love and what He has to do.

There is power in the name of Jesus. Just the near mention of His name sends demons running for cover like a bunch of cowards.

Never underestimate the power and love of ten Yorkies in a basket.

Real recognizes real, and the rest are caught in lies.

Listening to a dog chew food and lap water is one of the greatest joys in the world.

You're an evil man if you don't like little dogs.

Dolphins and whales like to swim and need space to live and breathe healthily, just like humans do. It's a crime to have them trapped in mini pools to perform stunts for human pleasure.

Albinos are God's special animals.

There is nothing more powerful and majestic than an albino bald eagle.

Albino peacocks are a symbol of divinity.

To see a pink dolphin is a rare blessing.

We have a great connection to all animals on this planet, and it's a shame not to use these potential energies and connect to them all.

Too many whales are dying from plastic bag ingestion. If you can help save the oceans, go and try to do it. And if you're not by an ocean, you can always help by throwing away street trash that you find along your journey.

Never put a Bible under your pillow.

When you're on fire, it is important to drink a glass of water.

It's not cool to play a fool; you're only hurting yourself and destroying your creditability.

Sometimes, a good laugh can cure all.

Everyone in a tribe has a role, just like the body of Christ has different parts.

The secret to our lives is hidden within our childhood drawings. It's important to save the early artwork of a child.

Bring love, or don't come.

People who don't want children are missing out on some of God's greatest blessings.

It is a curse to say you're not worthy.

Abortions should be illegal. If you had one, you definitely need deliverance from it.

It takes wisdom to excel in life; get as much of it as you can. Pray for it to find you.

Some people can't find forgiveness in their hearts. There is only bitterness that rules their actions. Healing can never take place with these emotions. Learn to forgive, and you will have peace.

The truth will set you free. Lies will enslave you.

Our Father in heaven wants us to have faith, hope, and love at all costs.

A little bit of faith can sometimes move mountains.

You must drop shame like a bad habit, or it will be the death of you.

You are love, you are worthy, and yes, you can do it.

Positive reinforcement always goes well with gentle love.

A gentle love will always win. Always.

You may spread His love like gentle rain in the spirit of a crying dove.

Team good will always triumph over the forces of darkness. Where there is light, there is love, and darkness can't live in the light; it dies in it.

It's up to you to make your dreams come true, but you're always going to need God's love to help.

There is nothing greater than God.

The breath of life is a gift from God. We can't survive without it.

The path of excess can lead to enlightenment, but it takes taking a path filled with disgrace and many failures that will ultimately hurt you more than you know.

There are always a few regrets in one's life. Try not to revisit them too often and do away with the pain they caused you if possible. Dwelling on negativity is not healthy for the soul.

The devil is a liar and an all-around poor sport. A total buzzkill. I'd love to hear him repent for all the rotten things he's done.

Everything exists because everything is.

God tends to the righteous and the wicked.

The faster you run, the harder you'll fall.

There have been many kings who have lost God's favor.

Women who are fair to look at set traps to catch men's eyes.

Women who are fair to look at struggle to find a truthful man.

Have respect for other religions; we are all on earth together.

Satanic temples should not be able to function as a religion. They are the antireligion. Pray for them; they need it the most.

People fear things that they can't understand. Take time to get the full picture before rushing to judgment.

People don't like to be around people who are more successful than them. There are many haters.

Someone who avoids answering a question is hiding their failure.

Never make fun of or talk ill about anyone who works harder than you.

When you use your spiritual eyes, there's nothing you can't see or figure out.

The spirits are everywhere you go and exist on many different seen and unseen levels of reality. You're never alone.

It's good for the soul to have a good cry every once in a while.

God is everything and everywhere; there is no escape from the eyes of the Lord.

People need their people high, but the wise seek solitude.

Always set impossible goals, and never stop trying to achieve them.

Proverbs

You will always be a success if you apply your best effort.

Always pray for a great vision; one day, God will bless you with one if you deserve it.

Talk to Jesus. He always hears you.

There are many strange and beautiful creatures in heaven.

The light of God sustains all love and want. It's the most beautiful thing that exists in heaven. Everything is one. Energy is everything.

There is a handicapped dog named Henry Wee-Wheels. There is much to learn from him. He has the spirit of ten bears. Long live King Henry.

Laika, the Russian space dog, should never be forgotten.

Every artist has a pile of crap works. Many get made, but only a few get chosen.

Try to avoid vain people; their energy steals from yours with every word they say.

Be the calm to their storm.

Always help the weakest one.

A gentle tone of speech can usually stop the shouting.

Never have the same fight twice. Try to squash it the first time. It's not healthy to rehash old beef. Avoid the repetitive fight loops.

Give them whatever they want, no matter what it is. It's a blessing to do this. Aim to please.

Talking about the faults of an ex-lover is like watching twenty horror films back-to-back. It only leaves you bitter. Focus on what went well instead. You can't turn back time.

It's okay to eat meat, but if you can become a vegan, it's even better for the soul.

Try and surround yourself with happy-minded people. No Negative Nancys.

Try not to cut anyone from your life, but look for a positive way to reconnect. There's more to gain.

Being too proud is a folly.

Humble yourself before you wreck yourself.

A soft word from the Holy Spirit is worth more than all the oil in the world.

When the going gets tough, eagle up and take crap from no one.

Sometimes, you might have to give someone an eagle grip to help them out of their own misery.

When the rivers open, there's no turning off.

Love the unlovable.

When falling in love, take your time. Wine is finer with age, and only fools rush in.

Sometimes, you have to do your duty and take one for the team.

Don't get trapped in the letter O.

Having good visual and mental projections is a gift from God.

It's good to practice meditation.

Make an effort to read a book.

The end is always closer than you think; don't give up.

"The concept of money is modern-day slavery. Why do we pay to live on a planet we're born on?" (Alien Wisdom).

Only speak the truth at all times; lying is devious with ill intentions.

Being a womanizer is a sickness.

Beware of women who have the spirit of flirt; they can't be trusted.

God does not favor whoremongers.

God dislikes those who practice witchcraft and magic.

Don't believe everything you hear. There are many out to de-

Proverbs

ceive you.

Everyone is a sinner. Jesus was the only perfect one, and He died for our sins.

Trash Island is mankind's worst shame.

Take a side on an issue; don't be lukewarm in your actions, or you'll never grow.

No risk, no reward; take a leap of faith.

You can do the impossible with God.

You must have the faith of a mustard seed.

Daily walks are good for the heart and add longevity to your life.

Drugs can only bring you so far; you will need God if you're trying to reveal the true mysteries of life.

Your phone is a false sense of security.

It is good to always wear clean clothes.

Don't wear the color black all the time; it will suck your energy in subconsciously.

Just remember, there is always someone out there who is bigger and worse than you and who will not show you the slightest bit of respect toward your feelings. Be cautious of a true gangster; he is rooted in evil intentions, and destruction is always in his path.

Pray for people in jail; they need it the most.

Only a fool calls himself a junkie.

Keep a good balance in all that you do. Don't fly too high or sail too low.

Never pay a stranger to hear your problems; that's why you have friends and family.

Take a good look at your eyeballs when you're in the mirror. They never lie to you.

To catch a thief, you sometimes have to play dumb.

Waves never stop crashing toward the shore, just like a fool never stops changing his opinions in a story.

There's only so much you can listen to when you're in a room full of junkies. Remember, you can always leave through the door you came in by to save your sanity. There's no shame in pulling an Irish goodbye at this point. It will only help you regain your own peace of mind and not ruin the rest of your day and night.

You should pray for every single person you see.

God speaks through the words of our grandparents.

Boycott the spirit of jail.

Try almost everything once; the more experience you have, the greater your wisdom shall be.

Only God can bring you true freedom.

When you feel the Holy Spirit working within you, seize it and do more of the activity that brought it there in the first place.

Future dreams are a blessing from God. They are trying to tell you something, so pay close attention to the details. If you have problems remembering, just hit the recall button in your brain.

With great wisdom comes great responsibility.

If everybody prayed, we wouldn't have wars.

Going to church is important because it is powerful to worship together, and it keeps together a good community.

We are all in this together; consider your neighbor no different than yourself.

When you use the word n*****, you're allowing the concepts of slavery to reenter the environment you're in, as well as society in general.

Demons get you to use foul language to get you to demoralize everything. Be wary of men who curse a lot; there is usually a demon attached to his words and thoughts.

To say someone's stupid is to put a curse upon them.

Proverbs

Hate and dislike are two very different concepts. Try not to hate anything.

There is nothing more dangerous than a man who has nothing to lose.

There is a lot of nonsense and uncertainties that clog our brains sometimes. Pray to God to help put you on a clear and straight path.

A lily in the field is smarter than the thoughts of ten men.

Bring peace to your arsenal of weapons.

Those who can't have children should consider adopting one. There are plenty of children who need families, and there are many blessings to be had from this path choice.

Money is the root of all evil.

There is always more room to love and to share, just like there's always more room for Jell-O.

The path to heaven cannot be bought.

Nothing says "I love you" like a big bear hug.

Humans sometimes act like vultures.

I've never seen a camel go through the eye of a needle.

Metatron was once human; he's a good role model.

Do not look at the clock during church. It is not important.

We constantly seek approval from our fellow man; without it, our lives are pointless.

You should read the Bible daily, even if you only have time for one small chapter. Get some in where you can at least once a day.

Every step we take forward, we push backward.

If you always do what everyone says all the time, you will lose your soul. Be yourself.

Speak with authority. Know what you say.

It's okay to have pleasure in this lifetime. Just keep it within reason.

Humans have so many emotions; try and master them all but don't get swept away in any one track of mind for too long. Switch styles and keep it moving fresh.

Try to avoid tares on the wheat.

Don't listen to negativity; tune it out and leave the conversation; you'll live longer.

Support those who come with happy favors.

Grow into the person God wants you to be. It may take time to find out what that is, but you'll know when you arrive at the correct answer.

Seize the day; try and catch a walk at sunset.

Native Americans have some Christian beliefs too.

It's good to be well-rounded and knowledgeable of all religions. Study more.

Take time with a wounded heart and do extra listening.

Your desires can lead you down the wrong path. Don't want anything too much except God's love.

If something has been eating at you all day, pray hard upon it to find a resolution.

Do not overeat, and don't be a glutton.

People who are envious are usually lacking in some form of love. They want what they can't have.

There is a time to celebrate; enjoy it while it lasts.

Repentance will help you to regain favor with the Lord.

Nobody likes a sore loser. Take it in stride, and learn from your mistakes.

Be slow to anger.

If you can't forgive yourself, how do you expect anyone else to?

Never say you're not worthy. It's a curse to say this.

Having a conversation with someone is a good way to take your

Proverbs

mind off the negative things that are holding you back.

Be prepared and always plan ahead. You don't want to get stuck unprepared when it's crunch time.

Having a creative journal is a good form of self-therapy and can come in handy in times of distress.

Happiness comes when you please the Lord.

Keep your hands to yourself; it is disrespectful to touch everything.

Be wary of people who always try to one-up you. This is vain behavior.

Work hard at whatever the job is.

It is good to feed strangers. A full stomach equals full love.

To get a trumpet to blow in heaven for you is an honor beyond proportion.

Angels rejoice when a sinner reverses his ways.

In heaven, there are creatures with multiple eyes.

When you're on the wire, and things become serious because everyone is eagerly watching, every thought counts, and you better come correct. The Holy Ghost knows all and will reveal it if necessary.

Humans do silly things and make tons of mistakes, but it's how we recover from them that is important.

Some comics have the ability to make one laugh. This is a blessing.

A great song is a song that even your grandmother would appreciate.

Children tell it as it is. They are very blunt about everything. There is a lot to learn from a child's answers.

Break up and try to stop a fight at all costs, even if that means getting in the middle.

Gang warfare and street beef are buffoonery rooted in evil. Try to avoid getting caught in the devil's gang.

Never tell someone you don't like their art, but always find something to compliment it by offering positive reinforcement.

Find something good in everything. Even the bad has something positive in it.

Always look on the bright side of life.

We need God's love like we need sunshine.

Always pray for someone to have a spiritual breakthrough.

To be able to make objects reappear in the dream world and to return to them is a good sign of spiritual growth.

Pray for those who don't dream.

Dreaming is more important than going to college.

Always pay your respects to those who have just crossed over. Go to their wake or service if they have one, and always offer prayers for them in the afterlife.

It's a jungle out there; it's good to know all animal calls.

There are locks and chambers everywhere you go. Your mobility, growth, and freedom depend upon how much access you have to them.

A tree blowing in the wind can become the joy of your day. Listen to what it says.

A good friend will always have your back, even when you're wrong.

There is nothing more soothing than a light, gentle rain on your face.

It's important to collaborate with others; there is more to gain when we work together.

God knows the number of hairs on your head.

If you're not having fun or finding happiness, it's probably not worth doing it, and you should quit.

Always try to read Scripture when you wake up and before you go to bed.

Having the Bible as the last words of the day before you go to sleep is healing and will help you sleep better.

Let go of regret; you can't turn back time, and it does no good to hold on to should-haves, could-haves, and would-haves.

Become like a child when doing joyful work. Hold a playful innocence.

Become ambidextrous if you can. Try and develop both sides of your brain. Use the hand you're not favored with to do simple tasks to help grow the other side. It's a shame that schools and society favor the development of only one side. If you are ambidextrous, you will have a great advantage in life. Try to cross the brain waves. Once you open both sides, that is when the real magic happens. Try it and see.

Something hanging upside down is usually a satanic act.

Be wary of people who dance with snakes or put snakes in their music videos. This is a satanic act. Serpent worship is bad mojo and not looked favorably upon by God.

Voodoo dolls are demonic by nature.

God can make all your goals come true.

If you're finding it really hard to concentrate, you might be under spiritual attack; recognize the signs and change your consciousness.

Your prayer is your sacred art.

Most artists are starving, but they hold other treasures.

It is important to save the cherished objects of the deceased to keep their spirit alive.

Keep pushing the limits of what's known; a tireless effort will find success in the end.

All glory goes to God, always and forever.

If someone has no family to be with or count on, be the family he doesn't have.

Take extra special care of the handicapped and those with disabilities.

Bring Scripture to a spiritual battle; it will be your best weapon.

Sometimes, it takes days to fight a battle, so know how to raise your energy levels so that you won't get tired quickly.

Objects in mirrors may be closer than what they appear.

Traveling is good for the soul and promotes spiritual growth. Try and have a trip planned in the future to some place you've never been before.

You know when you're lying to yourself; try to avoid this behavior. The truth will set you free.

If you're tired, pull the car over and take at least a ten-minute nap. It's better than crashing.

Get plenty of rest before you go to work; there's nothing worse than fighting sleep on the job. It's disrespectful to your boss and coworkers and just plain unproductive in general.

Fight the good fight for life.

Do what your boss tells you to do, and don't complain.

If you're tired, sleep.

Be cognitive and always know the time and date.

Bees are sacred; do not kill one of them.

Practice safe sex.

If you can, save sex for marriage. It will mean more, and it shall be more holy.

There are truths, and there are absolute truths, and then there are lies. Deal with the absolute truths.

Don't get trapped by time; always allow some free space in your life.

Always take at least a couple of minutes a day to enjoy being outside. This is healthy for the soul.

Without Jesus's love, we cannot get into heaven.

You have to be prepared to go the extra mile when someone is suffering from demon overload. Stay in constant prayer and do what you can to try and change their situation.

If someone is spiritually lost, that's all the more reason to look for them.

Picking a fight with the devil is extremely dangerous and can cost you your life if you're not completely fortified and protected by the Lord and mentally stable as well.

Stop all the fighting of this and that, make peace with the world, and just spread and seek love, and then love will come to stay with you.

A wise man can never have enough wisdom.

Trying to take your life is one of the most selfish acts known to man. One should never lose hope like that. There is always hope. It exists on many levels if you're looking for it. Just look for it in these times of trouble, and you'll find it. The key is to look.

When the universe doesn't want you, tell it, "Jesus loves you."

If you're tired of making mistakes, don't make them anymore.

When all love is gone, it still exists. You can never lose it because God is love, and He's everywhere.

Hug a tree; trees love hugging.

The owls are angry we're cutting down the forests; they have no place to go anymore.

Turn those frowns upside down; Jesus loves you.

Borders separate us.

Learn to hold your fire in stillness.

If you can't see it, you can't be it. Visualize everything, then manifest it.

Don't take a soulless job just because the money is good. Deep down, you will not be happy.

Sometimes you feel the whole world's against you, pay no mind to strangers' demands. Be yourself.

Start each car ride with a quick prayer for a safe journey.

There is a time for music, and there is not a time for it. God makes time for everything.

Don't fall victim to useless chatter; you'll drive yourself crazy if you hear too much of it. Learn to keep a steady mind.

Free your mind from mental slavery. Sometimes, we're our worst enemy.

Be cautious about who you let into your circle of trust. Not everyone has your best intentions or knows how to love correctly.

If you can't be yourself, who are you?

A kind smile from a stranger can change your whole day around. Smile back.

You can't burn the candle at both ends; you'll only end up sick and tired.

Take things seriously when it's matters of the heart.

When your gut feeling says no, it's dangerous to push it. Stop yourself if you can.

There is nothing like a good company that warms the heart.

Actions speak louder than words.

A woman who will bring you a cup of water after you dance is a keeper.

It is possible to have great vision by dancing your heart out.

Be watchful and use wisdom wherever you go. Keep your senses up and ready for anything that comes your way at any time, night or day.

Listen to reason when it whispers to you.

People who say, "You're going to hell," are throwing a curse on you, and you cannot trust them; they don't hold your best interests at heart and are basically mean-spirited. Rebuke them quickly.

Keep heart in all things you do; never give up the good fight.

"Some choices are optional, and some are definite" (Henry Cook).

People who wear sunglasses are hiding more than just from the sun and have a disconnection from the world around them as well.

The quest for fame can never be filled by those with hungry eyes.

Working together brings peace and joy to the world most of the time. It brings harmony to any job or task at hand when you can achieve a common goal in unison.

May there be peace and love and perfection in all God's creations.

It is important to squash the beef.

The fall time is a good season for squash and reconnecting with a former lover.

It should be a goal to plant at least three good seeds a day.

One should hold a special place in their heart for war veterans, always thank them for their service and ask for their wisdom when you meet one.

Sometimes, we must get messy before we can get clean.

Usually, when you think you got it all figured out, that's when you realize you know nothing at all, and you are like a baby again.

You should never have to beg for something you want. It should be given to you if you want it bad enough, and you deserve it.

Beggars usually say, "God bless you." That's more than I can say for most people you meet. What a nice way to thank someone by throwing a good blessing of the Lord their way. More people need to do this in their daily routines and interactions.

Never be embarrassed or too timid to say "God bless you" to someone.

There is always something to learn from the words of a homeless man. Usually, they are not as crazy as people tend to think.

It is a blessing to speak in metaphors.

You usually never say something about someone that doesn't apply to yourself as well.

Keep balance at all costs.

Never be afraid to tell someone when they're out of line; you can save their life, and they will respect you more for telling them in the end.

A state of nirvana can be achieved through the use of multiple joyful acts.

When you see a giant face on the face of the mountain you're climbing, you know you've achieved something great. Go as high as you can get; conquer all fear.

People are more animalistic when they congregate in mobs.

It is good to protest peacefully and nonviolently as Gandhi and Martin Luther King Jr. did. Nothing gets solved or achieved when people start burning things down or looting stores. That is something they like to do in hell.

To try and understand God's love is just mind-bending.

Martin Luther King Jr. wanted us to have faith, hope, and love for all mankind.

Gandhi was a Christian too.

"The only tyrant I accept in this world is the still small voice within" (Gandhi).

Proverbs

Always want to sit up front, you learn more.

One can learn a lot about true love by watching John and Yoko together. They were the embodiment of true, pure love.

Kiss with a shyness.

A woman who knows how to feed a man is worth her weight in rubies.

True love is never having to say you're sorry, but you should anyway.

You can never trust a woman who's a gold digger; her ways are rooted in greed.

Always root for the underdog; when he triumphs, there is great joy.

If you're going to speak to someone, make sure you are always speaking clearly; mumbled words cause mixed feelings.

Don't half-ass anything. Go the distance

There is a scientific method and a spiritual method of looking at illness. One is based on how much medication to give, and one is based on your faith in God. Doctors are usually misinformed due to a lack of spiritual knowledge. Finding God is the answer to all your problems.

Hard times may come and go, but a loyal woman will stick through them all. Pick the right lover.

Most jokes aren't that funny.

Never lie or cheat your lover; if you do, the relationship will usually end.

Serious words come from serious men.

We usually work and live in certain patterns and cycles; try to break the cycles, and never get stuck in one pattern in order to allow yourself to spiritually grow faster. It's good to mix it up.

Love the ones who love you and love the ones who hate you too.

To see the sun falling out of the sky is a horrible sight, and I hope you never see this.

The book of Revelation shows how mighty and powerful God is. Praise and fear the Lord.

Playing chess will teach you how to plan for a better future.

Give respect where respect is due. Don't be disrespectful.

Thinking and doing it are the same thing. Be careful about what you think about.

There's more to life than just scrolling though people's lives and hitting like buttons.

There are many eyes in heaven, and they are always watching.

Try and be merry and in good spirits, freedom comes from a joyful heart.

Always be grateful; never forget what it took for you to get there. You must have gratitude.

Never say anything bad about the Holy Spirit; that is one sin that's not forgiven.

Don't doze off during church; it's rude.

There is nothing like the female members of a church to make the spirit fly.

When you take communion, remember the significance of the blood and the body of Christ.

You shouldn't take communion if your heart and spirit aren't in it completely.

Sing a song of praise in the company of others. Pass along the good vibrations.

Jesus loves even the black sheep.

Make positive suggestions; avoid negative solutions.

When you're on the wire, getting a repeat of the words can sometimes kill your spirit. Embrace the correction the first time, and you'll live a bit longer.

Never be too needy that you drain someone's energy; nobody likes an energy sucker.

God has a plan for everything.

God got the idea for man's hair from the grass that grows.

There is value and power in the blood; that's why witches try and sacrifice with it.

Eve could hear the serpent talk.

There are three things that hold great spiritual power for you: Scripture, fasting, and prayer. Use them all.

"He who moves a mountain begins by moving little stones" (Chinese proverb).

Faith can move mountains.

Building faith is like a blind man walking up a staircase.

Demons will try to steal your birthright as well as other sacred things if you let them get that far. Stop sinning.

Sugar can develop into a spiritual snake problem in your veins and can lead to serious illness if abused.

Crack is wack; just say no.

If you're unsure of something, pray on it till you get an answer.

If you cannot tell the truth, you are a coward.

Wars were fought because someone was called a coward.

Anal sex is an act that is rooted in filthy lust.

It's an act of extreme love when you are able to change a grown man's diaper for him.

Be cautious when dealing with people who have snake or Grim Reaper tattoos; destruction follows them.

Evil tattoos on one's body can be a gateway to demonic enslavement.

God has a plan for everything; you must believe in his judgments.

Religion can be like surfing a one-hundred-feet wave. You need help to get toed in, but once you are there, it's one heck of a ride for those who dare.

There is nothing worse than wasted talent.

You can find happiness everywhere you look; it's all about perspective.

You can tell a man by the company he keeps.

Miracles happen all the time when you're on God's path.

Most people will see a miracle and still won't believe it.

If you want to see miracles, go to church, and you'll find them there.

Church is a haven for all. Even the worst sinner is welcome within its walls.

Your church family are your brothers and sisters.

Demons hate the Holy Ghost fire.

When a demon manifests in someone, you must have faith in the Holy Ghost to help expel it.

Through your lips, give constant praise to God and Jesus.

You will never leave church saying that you didn't learn something new.

God grants safe passage through the dream world to those who deserve it.

If you get shot with a bullet or dart or arrow in a dream, it usually means you're under satanic spiritual attacks. You should rebuke these dreams as quickly as possible to reverse the curse.

Reverse the curse.

If you get up in the middle of the night from a bad dream, go have some milk and cookies and read some Scripture and rebuke that dream before you return to sleep again. You'll be in a better state of mind, and then you'll have less of a chance to reenter the same horrible concepts that you were just dreaming about. Knowing how to break an evil dream loop is an important skill. This is just one technique.

If you're really, really being attacked in your sleep state, and you have some bad boys on your every move, wake up and start reading Scripture and repeating prayers of warfare until you give it your all. Demons hate when you read Scripture, and they can't stand war prayers that protect you and your house. This just might work.

God is not going to save you every time. He has His reasons, and sometimes you must pay for your sins, and there's nothing you can say or do about it. I hope this never happens to you. It's hands down the worst thing in the world. But you still must keep hope alive at all costs, or else you're going to be a dead man. Hard-core repenting sometimes can save you in this situation if you're lucky.

Memorize the twenty-third psalm by heart and know it so well that you can even recite it when you're sleeping. It just might save your life one night and avoid a fight. Demons hate the twenty-third psalm. It's a special wartime prayer you should know by heart.

Pray to have all your house, its belongings, your bed, your pet, and your family covered in the blood of Jesus for protection against evil spirits. And pray for this in the name of Jesus. What you pray for in His name will happen; it's a promise. There is power in the name of Jesus.

It's always good to take nature breaks and listen to the trees talk.

Finding wisdom is like doing a jigsaw puzzle; it's all about making the right pieces fit together to form the greater picture.

"Prayer is the key of the morning and the bolt of the evening" (Gandhi).

Be a "Yes, I can," not "I think I can't."

Moving little stones is easy because they are so little.

Step by step, walk towards greatness.

You can heal your body with a breath of life. Where life exists, death will cease to exist. Practice your breathing meditations and direct the oxygen to the ill parts of your body. Have it surround the darkness, and then when you exhale, you release all the excess not needed from your body. This is a good healing technique.

Repeating the same folly is like throwing salt on open wounds.

Don't ever glorify demonic behavior. There is no honor in that.

Don't jump to conclusions fast; always hear all the evidence to make a fair judgment.

If you hear something so many times, you'll start to believe it. Don't fall victim to this.

Sometimes, it takes an oddball to make sense of what's normal.

Have complete faith in your Father in heaven. He wants your all.

Have remorse for the diving horse.

A heart emoji is a cheap way to say you love something; a call voice to voice goes so much further.

If you want to be a hero, tell people that Jesus saves.

God has the power to heal you in a millisecond, no matter what the illness. Pray for healing with all your heart, and never stop. Miracles have been known to happen.

Be a part of the solution, not the problem.

Philippe Petit could not have danced in the sky over the World Trade Center without a strong super faith in God.

God showed up on the morning of 9/11. Many great miracles were performed on a grand scale. Many found religion on that day.

Fear this and fear that, but you should only fear the Lord and not finding His love.

Pray for even the evilest of men. Prayers and love can change one's heart for the better. They need it the most. Never underestimate the power of prayer and what it can do in any situation.

It's hard to concentrate when you have one hundred haters praying for your downfall.

The mind rules the body, so keep both healthy.

Dogs are a man's best friend. They love you when you're at your best and love you even more when you're at your lowest. There is much to learn from a dog.

They have pills that can do just about anything, but there's not one that can build your faith in the Lord.

Take the road less traveled.

Conspiracy theories only instill fear and paranoia, and who needs that?

Look busy; Jesus is coming.

Justice is always sweet when served correctly.

Guilt can swallow a man whole.

Keep knocking on heaven's door, and it shall be opened.

Sometimes, you need a cup of quiet.

Keep jumping toward heaven; one day, you just might reach it.

God instills fear into those who are in need of change.

There is nothing more dangerous than a man who has nothing to lose.

Wicked tongues and attitudes sometimes come with a smile.

Salvation comes by the grace of God.

Everyone has a price, and most sell out quickly when under extreme pressure. Save your soul, don't be a sellout.

Rats are common among thieves.

Do something great; dare to go where none have gone.

No one ever said life was easy; work harder.

Believe you can achieve it all.

What goes up must come down.

"Goonies never say die" (Chunk)

Victory is sweeter than honey.

God decides who wins and who loses.

The heart has a will of its own.

Find a good rock to build on.

Never quit on your blessings; it could be around the next corner. Be persistent in your goals and actions.

When the sun falls out of the sky, you better hope you're one of the chosen.

Quality, not quantity.

Quantity, not quality.

Have fun, or it's not worth doing it.

Keep it simple; don't overdo it.

When writing a poem, it can be good or bad, but it's the quest there within that counts.

Don't try to dominate every situation you're in. It's okay to be submissive sometimes.

Becoming a better lover is a series of trials and errors.

When people are trying to call you, pick up the phone; you could just save someone's life; you never know. Obviously, they wanted to connect with you for a reason. Don't be cold unless it says spam risk; then, it's okay to not pick up.

Take responsibility for your own actions as well as the ones you're with.

There's always something more you can do for someone; don't quit on them just because you don't want to get your hands dirty.

Good love is sharing a meal with someone.

Don't be rude to your host; always eat what is offered to you.

Always try to clean and eat everything on your plate. Don't

waste food.

People who do drugs usually die at an early age.

Spend a lot of time thinking about how you'd like to be remembered when you pass away. This will help you figure out what you need to do while you're still alive.

The phrase "Only the good die young" is a lie; people who live long lives are just as good.

Never be so drunk that you can't handle a crisis situation if one shall occur.

You'll usually find foolish behaviors or conflicts at the end of long stories.

Try to use the hand you don't normally use to do simple tasks more often. It's beneficial to learn to use both sides of your body.

Rock is a symbol of hope.

God can build His house upon the rock.

To see a white dove fly across the night sky is a blessing.

The modern man is obsessed with squares; try thinking in circles for a change.

You won't get bullied if you have a lot of heart for what you do.

Never fight with your best friend; it kills the soul.

Birds of a feather flock together.

Don't blame other people for your mistakes.

All the wisdom in the world can't turn back time to fix mistakes but can be used to help craft a better future.

Try not to repeat the same mistake twice; only a fool repeats folly.

You can take a hundred showers and never wash the shame away; what you need is deliverance.

Grinding your teeth can be a demonic attack.

Shame can sting worse than thirteen wasp bites.

Shame and guilt go hand in hand. They are a tag team of disaster.

Reach a point in life where you don't need the comfort of others in order to have a good time; be more self-sustaining.

There is a spirit in the snowfall that is more soothing than ten suckling babies.

The first snow of the year is always holy.

People say that they're enjoying the hot weather and that they're glad there's no more snow, but boy, are they completely wrong. We need the snow and cooler temperatures, or else we'll fry on earth.

All the microwaves from cell phones and satellites can't be good, and it's affecting our overall health and the way we think. We're permanently on vibrate, and we don't even know it. Try not to keep your cell phone in your front pockets, which are near your private parts. It can cause impotence.

Where there's big money, there's big crime.

If the top three richest people in the world got together, they could build enough bread factories around the world to stop world hunger.

Not all Russians hate Ukrainians or want this horrible war.

Keep your eye on the prize; you can't get what you cannot see.

To say you're going to call someone back and then not do it is an insult.

The spirit of murder finds those who possess firearms.

Don't talk over the radio when they are trying to land the plane.

"Are you happy today, Peter?" This is a good way to start a conversation, and it is the first thing Peter will say to you when you see him out and about. It gets you every time. Love for Peter.

Everything is everything.

Don't ever tell someone to shut up; just ask them politely to be quiet.

Proverbs

You can't get a badger out of its hole. It's too strong.

It is always respectful to ask someone's permission before taking their photo.

Being bitter is like when a snake bites you in the butt. Stay positive.

Sometimes, not even gravity can pull you down. You must fly like an eagle.

Spiritual energy and spirits are everywhere; it's possible to see them depending upon where your energy level is at, but most of the time, it's invisible to the human eye. Raise your inner frequencies.

Always pray for better hearing and better vision.

Always be fair when paying someone's wages for their work.

The way of the transgressor is a hard and vigorous road.

"Just be who you are; they can never take that from you" (Coleman).

Not all things were meant to be told. Sometimes, it's up to you to figure it out.

Faith begins where fear ends.

We're so quick to judge. This is a disgusting behavior. Slow your roll and be rational with your thoughts.

Do you see all the vanities? They're not hard to spot. Too much pride is not a good thing.

If your heart gets dirty, pray for a clean one.

Be careful of written or verbal traps, as springes to catch woodcocks.

It's hard to hear with all the corn in your ears.

Foolish wisdom is like tears from a clown.

The great floods came and went, and everything perished, but the rock remained.

Rock came before the olive branch.

When you're in nature, don't use your phone.

Go fishing sometime; maybe God will let you catch a fish.

One man's trash is another man's treasure.

Someone once said that the more keys one man has, the less important he is. This was a lie.

It takes courage to build faith.

Complete surrender. That is the mission.

Soon, there'll be a man sinning on Mars.

It should be a daily goal to try and do at least three productive things a day. It will help you to stay on the right track and to become successful.

Ask not what God can do for you but what you can do for God.

Tune in; drop in.

Everybody will be unfamous for fifteen minutes.

Whenever you have a bad thought, say, "They'll be none of that!" And it will rebuke it with quickness.

If you see a miracle, make sure you tell someone about it so that you can share in God's greatness.

Everybody's always looking for a sign from God; well, look no further than the breath you take. For everyone is a sign of God's love.

Peak at the right time if necessary, but don't overdo it.

Always remember to give thanks to the Holy Ghost. He's a hard worker.

God searches men's hearts and knows the truths within.

Pay attention when there are talks of wars; prophecy may be getting fulfilled.

Baptism.

The Lord is my rock.

When you say "I do" when you get married, you're taking an

Proverbs

oath under God, and what God binds should not be separated.

To do a spiritual battle, you must have the endurance of a polar bear swimming for ice.

Jesus is beautiful, like a wild horse running through a wheat field in the sunset.

Faith can even be found in dreams.

Hope can save you from making a bad decision.

Love is God's language. Learn to speak it.

Faith is the steps you take when you're not looking.

Hope, even in the smallest of doses, can change the world.

Love those who love you, and try to love those who hate you too.

Give thanks for the blessing of a quiet nap.

Try to have the affection of a mother elephant putting her trunk around her young.

Baby elephants are sacred creatures. To see one in a dream is a special blessing beyond proportion.

Hold the family values of a herd of elephants migrating across a desert searching for a watering hole.

There is an organ in heaven, and when it plays, it's so loud and powerful that you feel holiness in your bones.

There's a rave in heaven where angels sing over house music.

Hearing an angel sing is more beautiful than anything you can ever imagine. There aren't words that exist on earth to describe it.

When you believe in something, you're making it a truth within your existence. Believe in God. He is good all the time.

You can dress for success. Try and always look presentable.

When something feels right, this is when you will feel God's energy and the energy of the Holy Spirit's love all around.

Ask the Holy Spirit to clean you daily.

Don't quit on someone just because you don't like their habits; cutting someone off solves nothing.

Be the point at which two rivers meet.

Never think you are alone; you have guardian angels and soul guides who pray over you day and night.

Try to be conscious even in your dreams. There is so much to learn and do on the other side. Pray for this gift.

Keep focus on the task at hand, and never get distracted by your cell phone.

Try to give more to charities. They exist for a reason, and if you were in that position, you'd want someone to help you, too, right?

What's fair is fair; always come correct in all your dealings.

God can turn even the hardest of days into a peaceful melody.

Have the eye of an eagle when searching for holy connections.

Connect the dots. All points lead to God.

Jesus's love can be felt in a gentle breeze.

Love comes in many forms; don't be afraid to learn them all.

Always turn a negative into a positive somehow.

If your house burns down, build a better one.

Strike while the iron's hot.

Jump for Jesus.

Plan for success. Plan to have God on your side.

A sparrow in a tree does not worry about where its next meal comes from; God tends to all His needs. So don't you worry either.

There is nothing like the feeling when a project comes together and God gives you all the right pieces that fall into place. That is a gift from God.

Do it right the first time; take the proper steps for success.

A dog licks your wounds when you're hurt. Learn from this behavior.

Never forget your roots, where you came from, and what it made you into today. All the past molds the future.

Make love like a peacock. Make it a beautiful and majestic display of affection.

Gossip is like bringing dirt up from a water well.

Carry the load for your brother and give him the easy job.

Try not to become a critic unless you're giving out some positive reviews.

Healing starts with a belief in the Lord.

Join forces with those who are happy.

Stay creative at all costs. Your artistic works are important for spiritual growth. Keep pushing.

Saying you're not artistic and don't have a creative bone in your body is a crime. We all have the gift of creativity.

If a thief wants something so bad, then give it to him. His greed will destroy him in the end anyway.

Always try to be on time for all your appointments. It's rude to be late and leave people waiting for you. This is disrespectful.

The junkie is always the weakest link and is easily slaughtered by bald eagles.

A lion takes what he wants; who's going to stop the king of the jungle?

There are many ways of fighting a spiritual battle; sometimes, you must be a tiger and a dove at the same time.

"Ask, and it shall be given you; seek, and ye shall find; knock, and it shall be opened unto you" (Matthew 7:7).

Always serve yourself last.

Being in love within a good marriage will lengthen your days on earth and keep you young in heart and body.

Talking to a fool is like stubbing your toe on the corner of a desk really hard.

Curb your tongue, and you won't lose your thoughts.

If you're the first person talking in a conversation, you will most likely dominate the conversation. Don't let another person's thoughts poison yours before you can even get them out. Beat them to it, but on certain occasions, it is rewarding to let the other person dominate the conversation. Being a good listener is a good skill as well.

Look at the world with eyes of compassion. Cry like a dove.

Don't let your ego and pride kill a good deed.

If you lay in bed too long, your body will begin to fail you. Get up and get out and get something; keep it moving. God gave us legs for a reason. And if you're handicapped and can't use your legs, God will pave you another way; don't you worry.

Don't get trapped in the ghettos of the mind.

Remember to seal and lock all gates and doors to your brain with Holy Ghost fire and the blood of Jesus Christ to avoid a demonic break-in.

There's no honor in quitting.

When walking in God's path, you become a changed person. The old laws and rules you followed no longer apply. It's very difficult to go back to the set ways of the past; you will experience discomfort on many levels. You are evolving to become a better person. If people notice this change in you, this is a good thing. The quicker you let it all go, the better adjusted you will become to your new life in the body of Christ.

Everybody has a different function, just like there are different body parts that make up the body of Christ.

Having the gift of tongues is a blessing bestowed upon one from the Holy Ghost, and only He can help you decipher what it means as well. Consider it a blessing if you can speak or understand this unusual language.

"Thou shalt not bear false witness against thy neighbour" (Exodus 20:16). This is one of the Ten Commandments.

Idols are as useless as the material they're made from.

Words hold meaning and tend to manifest, so choose them wisely.

Regrets are like thieving monkeys, but they rob you from your soul.

A junkie can never save money.

The Bible is like a bomb of a very large firework. *Boom!*

God is the greatest gift giver in the universe.

Forgive and forget; those are great words to live by.

There are only so many hours in the day; you must set more quality time for the Lord.

Don't trust a man who can't give you a firm handshake after you meet him.

Find a good and wise wife with whom you can grow with God, and then watch as your problems disappear.

God must come first before every relationship.

Be the rock on which God can build His house.

A turtle's heart beats for five days after it dies. There is much to learn from the ways of a turtle.

If you want to learn about what happens to you when you die, just start watching videos of people's testimonies of when they flatlined. All find God in one form or another in the end, but some find a hellish existence. Could so many people be lying? This isn't a conspiracy; it's the truth.

Vanity is everywhere; always have a hawk's eye for these vain behaviors and try not to slip into them yourself.

If you don't love yourself, just know that Jesus loves you very much, and you can build on that.

Not all apple trees bear good fruit, and some are rotten with worms and must be tossed aside. But some are ripe and can be pressed to make sweet cider and apple pies for mass consumption.

People who root for the bad guy to win in movies are usually wicked by nature.

Everybody loves a good movie villain until you meet one in real life. Then it gets real, real quick.

Horror movies are the work of the devil and should not be watched or made.

Never underestimate your enemy; he's smarter than you think. Pray for him.

A wise man knows wisdom when he hears it, but to a fool, nothing even passes the loud drums in his ears.

Pray for a good harvest and bless the food at your local grocery store. Blessed food is important before consumption.

Make God happy. That should be your only agenda.

May the still voice guide you to greatness.

When someone says the milk is sour, it usually is. There is no need to try a sip. The same can be said for spiritual beliefs.

A man who has a lot of money will always live in doubt of things.

Trees are worth more than all the gold in the world.

Sloths have a tough time climbing over all the cut-down forest!

Don't be a should have, could have, or would have; take action.

When you see something's off, don't be afraid to say the right thing.

Make sure your actions stay humble at all times.

An evil woman can be as vicious as a poisonous viper.

Happy is the man who does right by the Lord and keeps His

Proverbs

laws.

What you see in dreams may come true; it's up to you to manifest it.

A good laugh is hard to come by, so enjoy it while it lasts. Laughter is a blessing from God.

Keeping faith is a permanent occupation.

Love those who love you back, and never forget to return a favor.

Committing adultery is like a form of spiritual suicide.

If you lose your way, repent, and don't leave a single sin out.

Don't be the dog with a monkey on its back.

Pets are our special friends; everyone should have at least one.

Keep thinking outside the box; don't get caught in its limitations.

Try imagining yourself soaring like the mighty eagle, then begin to fly.

Sometimes, we're our own worst enemy. Love yourself correctly and do the right thing.

God is perfect in all His judgments. Who are we to judge?

People who swear a lot are usually frustrated individuals and are holding the spirit of anger.

If you make a mistake, do your best to correct the situation.

Never curse the ones who love and support you.

True love is so rare, like seeing a pink peacock. When you find it, bask in its greatness for as long as possible.

Wear your heart on your sleeve so that everybody can see your intentions.

Giving away art is like giving a piece of your heart.

Have a ball, and be merry, just don't overdo it.

Freedom comes in many forms; some can even be dangerous.

The more possessions, the more worries.

In a world full of doubts, one must keep faith to survive.

If Jesus can give you a second and third chance, so should you.

If you want to soul search, try making art and see what comes out. It's extremely rewarding.

Making it to heaven should be high on your goal list.

Good wisdom is like a matched beat delivering a locked groove of rhythm.

Focus on God, and the rest shall pass.

"Love one another many, many times" (Pete Iuvera).

"God gave us free will; you don't like it, don't listen" (Scott Cotton).

Even a junkie has some wisdom if you can dig deep enough to find it.

Faith can be grown in the presence of synchronistic events; pay close attention to them when they happen to you and fall in your path.

Open your mind, and your heart will follow.

Try and be gentle in all your dealings.

Work with those who share common goals; that's where you'll do your best work.

Native Americans consider it an honor to give away their best possessions to others; this is a good trait to have. Always give your best one.

Reading good wisdom is like scoring a gggggggooooooooooooooooooooooooooooooooooooooaaaaaaaaaaaalllllllllllllllll in soccer.

Take a piece of art or drawing from a child or loved one and save it for years. Then, reunite it with him or her at an older age. There will be great joy and a blessing at that moment.

There is nothing that compares to the feeling when two neighbors come together with reason and understanding.

Proverbs

It is good to keep company with an old friend who loves you for all your rights and wrongs. Someone who knows your ins and outs and basically just loves you for being you.

Sometimes, we must cross a deep ocean to get to the dry land.

Spiritual breakthroughs can happen when you least expect it. Sometimes, the littlest of change can make all the difference in attitude and perception.

Let reason and rationalization rule your conversations. Slowly form your conclusions.

There is nothing in the world that can compare to the spirit of a mighty tiger who refuses to lose.

Find the path that equalizes friendships.

A stormy night can lead to a warming sunrise at dawn. New light will always bring forth a renewal of spirit.

It is not in our human nature to quit; we were built for survival.

Try and stay creatively motivated even when you lay in waiting.

The more sacrificed, the more earned. Go to the full distance necessary for success.

Sometimes, a clown is needed to chase a bull away.

Live and let live should be the only deer solution.

Be the word of wisdom for the ones who have none.

A witch lays her bed in wickedness while the righteous sleep with the Lord's favor.

A priest or pastor is like a father with wisdom.

For those who have no father on earth, just remember you have a Father in heaven who loves you very much, and He will love and guide you to goodness and understanding.

Love is your only job.

Good wisdom is like finding a pearl in an oyster.

Gravity can suck everything down but your spirit.

Be playful like a tiny bear.

Never come between a momma bear and her cubs; you will get touched.

You should try to paint a portrait of someone you hold fondly. This is a blessing that oozes with love juice and holds a great honor of affection.

Good seeds grow when you put God first.

Hard workers reap when the harvest bursts.

Try to express your love through a written poem, then watch as it manifests in your life and your words come alive and shower you with blessings.

There is nothing that can't be fixed with the love of the Lord.

"For the word of God is quick, and powerful, and sharper than any twoedged sword, piercing even to the dividing asunder of soul and spirit, and of the joints and marrow, and is a discerner of the thoughts and intents of the heart" (Hebrews 4:12).

Falling in love is easy; it's sustaining it that requires perseverance.

It's the love that keeps the love in perseverance.

Great love and great faith can make a blind man see again.

Great love and great faith can make a deaf man hear again.

"And now abide faith, hope, love, these three; but the greatest of these is love" (1 Corinthians 13:13, NKJV).

You may spread His love like a gentle rain in the spirit of a crying dove.

God's love can be found in a field of freedom.

God's love is in the books of the Bible; read them.

It is dangerous to quit on love; we need it to survive.

Love is the only thing we need to revive.

It's always okay to overdose on love.

Proverbs

It's love when you hear a mourning dove.
Love holds no price; it should be free.
Love is usually delivered with lots of glee.
Love is what it takes, so that is what you must give.
Love is the only way that one should live.
Love and joy can be found all over when you bathe yourself in good deeds.
Let love and joy suffice all of your spiritual needs.
Make love, not war.
Love is where the eagles soar.
Love crosses borders and can break down any tall wall.
Love is a cushion underneath, catching us when we take a good fall.
Love without ceasing.
Love is not leashing.
Let a gentle love have the final word in any disagreement.
Let gentle love be your agreement.
Love is a mission that's not impossible.
Love made Saint Jude do the impossible.
The more love you give, the more love you'll get.
The more love you get, the less you fret.
No time to be shy when you're in the tunnel of love.
The tunnel of love is the time for love.
Love is like a giraffe giving birth.
Love is worth all of the worth.
Love puts the ram in da Rama Lama Ding Dong.
Love makes every love song our song.
We must first fail at love before we can be successful with it.
Love is Michael Knight when he talks to his good friend KITT.
Finding love can be like drinking from the fountain of youth.

Richard Wislocky

Love to kick the truth to the young black youth.
When love enters your life, who's got room for hate anymore?
Love is when you knock, and then heaven opens its door.
Love thy Lord with all thy heart and soul.
Love is the guide that keeps you in control.
Love is patient like the sun at dawn.
Love is like the waking of fawns.
Love will always put you on the right path.
Love is tender and has no wrath.
Cherish the love in your life.
Love is a rare bird of paradise.
Love is like the rebar of a giant skyscraper.
"Love saves the day" on the front of a newspaper.
Love saves the day, every day, if you love it.
Love takes this rotten job and shoves it.
Put your love to the test; how deep can it show?
Put your love in a nest; see how far it can grow.
Keep love playful like a panda bear in heat.
Keep love playful on all the city streets.
Many people danced at the Love Parade.
Many loved hugging during an air raid.
Hate cannot grow where love takes root.
Love is giving someone an old pair of boots.
Love the fight and the struggle for good.
Love is the best; this is understood.
Love can be found; it's never that lost.
Love can be found without a cost.
Love can be seen when you're facing a mirror.
Love for the Father when He makes our dreams clearer.
Love can be heard when a mourning dove cries.

Proverbs

Love can be found where a hibernating bear lies.
Love can't be bought; it's worth more than money.
Love can sometimes make a good funny.
Love is so kind, like a deer by the river.
Love is the jacket on a Yorkie, so it doesn't go shiver.
Love is divine, a gift from our Father.
Love is worth it, always the bother.
Love will provide; it gives to the needy.
Love is patient and never greedy.
Love is not blind; it's meant for the seeing.
Love me two times, be double in seeking.
Love is in line, cross in the greening.
Loves on the mind, for it were left fiending.
Love till it shines, like the sun's glares gleaming.
Love on rewind, reflections left beaming.
Lovers will find, together we are dreaming.
Lovers subscribe, then comes receiving.
Lovers abide, joining and teaming.
Love is our pride when never scheming.
Love is a ride, a place to go to the meeting.
Love is a card full of joyful greetings.
Love is a drum, constantly beating.
Lovers embrace, a kiss to the face.
Love is on time, never a race.
Love is a find; open its case.
Loves combined, wedding white lace.
Love fills the place when it's with grace.
Love always pounds, thumping with bass.
Love plays a card, holding an ace.
Love sometimes burns, stinging like mace.

Love leaves a trail, one to be traced.
Love is permanent and can't be erased.
Love knows no shame and can't be disgraced.
Love is amazing and full of grace.
Love is the timing when keeping pace.
Love is the turtle that won the race.
Love is the smile that's stuck on your face.
Love is a dish, exotic with taste.
Love from the speakers, pounding with bass.
Love is a jewel stuck in a case.
Love is a base, never in chase.
Keep love in the heart; don't tear it apart.
Love is God's gift, sacred like art.
Love is a bullseye when hit by a dart.
Love is the filling, stuck in the tart.
Love is the food we put in the cart.
Love's not dumb; it's always smart.
Love is the sea that Moses part.
Love is the blood from Jesus' heart.
Love is Joseph and his coat.
Love is key that brings a good note.
Love is the words not stuck in my throat.
Love for the ram, the sheep, and the goat.
Love was Boaz thinking of Ruth.
Love to the children of all the young youths.
Love for good wisdom and all of its truths.
Love from a heater warming cold boots.
Love for tall oak and all of its roots.
Love for the dreamers who live in cahoots.
Love from the love boat when it goes and toots.

Proverbs

Love from a star when it goes shoots.
Love had Esther for her new king.
Love for the angels when they go sing.
Love for the future and what it brings.
Love for the honor of halo rings.
Love for the yan and the big ying.
Love from a dolphin when it goes ping.
Love for the gangle and for the ging.
Love for the bongo when it goes bing.
Loved it when Samson had all his hair.
Love from above where eagles stare.
Love for the polar and grizzly bear.
Love for the peoples from everywhere.
Love for Jesus and those who dare.
Love for just scales that balance fair.
Love for the doctors that really care.
Love for apples, oranges, and pears.
Love is gentle and never mean.
Love for the sober and the clean.
Love is a sunny sunshine beam.
Love for warm showers filled with steam.
Love of a king who needs his queen.
Love for the electric drum machine.
Love for the cheetah, sleek and lean.
Love for the junkies and the fiends.
Love for Noah and love for the ark.
Love is walking a dog in the park.
Love for the light and not for the dark.
Love is a birch tree pealing its bark.
Love for the singing song of a lark.

Love for cops and all the sneaky narks.
Love for the snakes and all of the sharks.
Love for Christ's body and parts.
Love for Jesus on the cross.
Love for the goldfish named Big Boss.
Love me some Indian secret sauce.
Love it when cheaters go and get tossed.
Love is a gentle sunny, snowy day.
Love will somehow pave a way.
Love is deep blue in a jay.
April showers love flowers May.
Love for what the father says.
Love E-ZPass and later go pay.
Love for the dancing Danny Kaye.
Love for fishing in the bay.
Just bring love and have a ball.
Love for the giraffe standing tall.
Love for Humpty when he had a fall.
Love for fountains in the shopping mall.
Love the Wolfpack when they call.
Love for mirrors in the hall.
Love for the leaves when they fall.
Love for you and for y'all.
Love for praying on my knees.
Love the maple and pine trees.
Love the coolness in the breeze.
Love for Russian and Chinese.
Love for David slinging rocks.
Love for athletes and the jocks.
Love for ticks that goes tocks.

Loves some noodles in the woks.

Love for angels that go knocks.

Love for keys that open locks.

Love the stillness when boats dock.

Love the Bible and what it's got.

You can never have too much love; seize it while it lasts.

Be an easy lover; don't make a fuss with the ones you love.

Put the word love at random throughout your artwork, and watch it grow.

Give love a second and third and fourth and fifth and sixth and seventh chance.

The lover of wisdom is, by definition, a philosopher, but a true lover of wisdom loves and fears the Lord, and yes, it's possible to love and fear at the same time.

Take all your potential love and make it into a kinetic love bomb. Then, drop it on the world.

All love crimes go into your spiritual jacket for later repentance.

Sowing the seeds of love is easy when you know where to plant it.

Don't be scared to receive love from a stranger.

Sometimes, you will have to fight for your love; stand up for what and who you love.

Try to imagine what your love will look like three years from now.

Give it your best, and nothing less than that.

The stronger your faith, the greater your joy will be in life.

Your faith is a shield in the armor of God.

The Bible is the Word of God.

People love to discredit the Bible when they haven't even read it; this is foolish behavior.

To fully gain knowledge of religion takes time and patience; there are no shortcuts. One must put in the work.

God and the Holy Ghost got a blind man and his dog, who were on the seventy-fourth floor of the World Trade Center, to safety on the morning of 9/11.

Faith is like bringing honey out of a bee's nest with no suit on.

Knowing when to keep something minimal and simple is a gift from God.

Hope is something that can never be let go.

Sometimes, we need help from our friends to figure out the proper course of action, and sometimes, we need the help of our family to figure out the proper course of action.

Any hour is a proper hour to host a Holy Ghost telethon when support is needed to be raised.

Be a good provider. Always be a step ahead when knowing a person's true needs. Do your best to bring them whatever they need before they even know they need it. This is good love.

Write and sing a song of affection to your lover. This is a sign of great affection.

Write a love poem to your lover and fill it with all of his or her virtues. This will be a sign of your constant devotion and admiration.

Once you find and fall into true love, you can never fall out of it. Love grows stronger in love, and God is true love.

Jealousy is like a double-edged sword that's thrust into one own self; it brings destruction to your soul.

It is impossible to be blind to morality when you have religious beliefs.

One cannot be spiritual without a belief or knowledge in God; the two go hand in hand.

Empathy must follow you in your actions and practices.

Positive kinetic energy, it's as simple as that.

On the path to enlightenment, we must first cross a river of filth.

When you're thinking about quitting, don't, but thrust yourself just a little bit extra. That will always lead to some reward of some kind.

Never give up on a fading friend.

When someone does something creative and artistic for you, it is rude not to show respect where respect is due.

There is nothing greater than when a dream comes full circle and manifests right before your eyes. This is a blessing from God.

When you pray, don't make it a big spectacle, and praying in privacy is always well received by the Lord.

There is a time and place when it is necessary to open the river.

When you get a taste of your own medicine, and something backfires on you, take it in stride and be thankful for correction. And don't feel so bad; medicine is healing.

Vultures feed on the words of the spiritual dead.

The truth does not and will never lay within the cards; this is only speculation.

There is nothing worse than a sick gambling addict. Pray for him.

All these Bitcoin and stock trading are just as bad as going to the casino. It's all a gamble and game that only the rich succeed, and they can only lead to spiritual poverty and corruption in the long run. Greed is greed. There is no get-rich-quick scheme that doesn't hold a spiritual price tag on it somehow.

"Thou shalt not covet thy neighbour's house, thou shalt not covet thy neighbour's wife, nor his manservant, nor his maidservant, nor his ox, nor his ass, nor any thing that is thy neighbour's" (Exodus 20:17). This is one of the Ten Commandments.

To put "In God We Trust" across dollar bills is a fallacy.

Sharing is caring.

Never be afraid to speak the truth.

It is never a good thing to call someone conceded.

Keeping heart is hard when it's racing at 120 bpm.

Always try to connect those who are separating from each other.

It takes a lot of responsibility to hold your fire with stillness.

You shouldn't smoke cigarettes around house pets; make an effort to keep it away from them if you are going to smoke.

Try to manifest your inner lion. It can come in handy when you're in a jungle. Everyone's got one deep, deep inside.

Try to manifest your inner turtle so that you can live a long and peaceful existence on earth. Everyone's got one deep, deep inside.

Don't drive so fast; there are animals trying to cross the roads.

Deer have a hard time crossing highways and become segregated into certain areas.

The song "Happy" by Pharrell Williams speaks a universal language that even your grandparents could understand. A good song will be respected by people of all ages.

"Always stay close to great spirit" (Native American commandment).

"Each one, teach one" (Henry Cook).

There are no accidents; there is only fate and destiny. God has a plan for everything; put your trust in the Lord.

Never settle for less than what you want, or you won't be happy.

Sometimes high expatiations may seem impossible, but nothing is impossible when you have the Lord's favor.

Give yourself a chance to think straight; don't subconsciously smother your objectives with negative thinking. Breathe and just be. Live and let live. It's in God's hands anyway.

People want to open your river and hold you to the wire; let them. You shouldn't hide anything from anyone. Always be just in your actions.

Don't let the threat of someone saying you're going to hell scare you into a state of unworthiness. This is the devil's trick to try and knock you down and stop you from achieving your goals.

Be one with God, and the rest will follow.

In harvest time, make sure you pick some peace.

Just bring love into your arsenal of weapons.

Always give back somehow; don't be frugal in your earnings.

The right prayer at the right time could make a world of difference to the outcome of any situation.

Love is sharing the knowledge you have with others in need.

Love is in the aftercare and the effort put therein. Don't ever quit praying for someone. Try and help their situation by being a steady and constant rock for them in times of need.

Pray for the ability to decipher voices, to know the good from the bad, because the devil sure is tricky sometimes. He can come disguised as an angel of light and make you believe the wrong thing. He will stop at nothing to disconnect you from God. And he's had years of practice too.

Everything stops when the Lord says stop, and everything goes when the Lord says go. God can heal you in a second if it's your time. Pray harder, and don't give up so easily. Your healing could be the next thing God just might do.

Obey the Lord, and you shall be happy.

When you have a good idea, jot it down quickly before you forget it.

Win some souls over for the grace of God, and it's your duty as a Christian to try your best at this.

Lead by example.

Try to manifest your inner shepherd and become a father or mother to a flock of many sheep. This is what God wants us all to do.

To be a good parent, you must be prepared to go the extra mile twenty-four hours a day, like a doctor waiting on call.

Hold your friends and family close to your heart, and never let go of them.

Your time here on earth is so little and goes so fast; use your time wisely.

When you don't have anything nice to say, don't say anything at all.

Put 120 percent effort into all that you do; stay focused on the mission at hand. You must be willing to give 120 percent.

If you're looking for success, success will find you. If you're looking for God, God will find you. The two go hand in hand.

All your efforts are always noted. They record, and they see everything you do in heaven in many books.

Bring yourself to a higher plain of consciousness, one where negativity does not exist. Drop the dead weight. It's easier than it sounds. You just have to try; that's the main thing.

It's always a good skill to be a good gardener; knowing when and where to plant is important.

Before you go to sleep, tell yourself to wake up consciously on the other side when you fall asleep. That way, when you do fall asleep, you will wake up, and you'll have total control. This is a good skill to have, and it's so easy to do. Just tell yourself to wake up on the other side, and you will. And always pray to God for a good vision. He will help you if you ask Him for help.

"Remember the Sabbath day, to keep it holy." (Exodus 20:8). This is one of the Ten Commandments.

Make hugs, not war.

Have the faith of a mighty oak tree.

Stay grounded in the belief that the impossible can be possible with the love of the Lord.

All roots need the water of Christ.

Let the actions of Jesus quench your thirst.

Help one another find a positive solution; teamwork is good work.

Having no competition is a good way to remain equal with your neighbor.

If you fall off your horse, pick yourself up again.

Hold the fire for those who can't.

A little here and a little there, and before you know it, you'll have a lot. Keep pushing.

Giving yourself to the Lord is like feeling the breeze from sticking your head out the window of your car's sunroof.

Hope can be found in a call from a good friend.

Faith can come from a state of surrender.

Try to be the bearer of good news; spread joy whenever you can.

Leave the forbidden in the passing dust.

Always turn your cell phone off in church.

Church is sustaining and full of fruit.

Church is like a steel toe construction boot.

Church puts together the missing pieces to the jigsaw puzzle.

Church brings words unleashed and never muzzled.

Church is where dreamers meet.

Church is where we Jesus seek.

Church is a rock within your foundation.

Church has the power to influence a nation.

Church is where we go to supercharge the spirit.

Richard Wislocky

Church is the place where we go to hear it.
Church is rewarding for those who seek it.
Church is a safe house for those who need it.
Church is holy, sacred, and kind.
Church is the place that polishes voices to shine.
Church is where we leave our problems.
Church is full of tons to go and solve them.
Church has the answers for those in need.
Church is the place where they always feed.
Church is rewarding, like knowing the seasons.
Church is the first 120 reasons.
Church is key to weekly good blessings.
Church is where lovers begin their wedding nestlings.
Church is where we go to give praise to our Father.
Church is worth all of the bother.
Who needs therapists when you have church?
Who needs evil when you have church?
Church is a place where we yearn to be humble.
Church garden flowers are where the bees stay bumble.
Church replenishes the tears of our sorrows.
Church takes care of todays and tomorrows.
Church has the power to conquer the darkness.
Church is the light that settles over darkness.
Church is the gift that just keeps on giving.
Church is breathing and constantly living.
Church is the place for spiritual gatherings.
Church brings togetherness and never scatterings.
Church is a breath of fresh air.
Church is for those who, in faith, go dare.
Church does good things for the hood.

Church is built out of bricks or wood.
Church can be majestic and mighty.
And some churches are sometimes really tiny.
Church always brings out the very best.
Church is where we spiritually nest.
Church is where we yearn to do good.
Church is where the unknowing becomes understood.
Church is a collective where two or more gather.
Church is the place that solves the matters.
Church is where we leave our problems.
Church is the place of let's go solve them.
Church is a shelter for the spiritually needy.
Church can never ever be greedy.
Church is a place that's full of solutions.
Church is a place that never is disillusioned.
Church can turn a whole day blessed.
Church is where the weak find rest.
Church has the ability to spread God's Word.
Church is the place, haven't you heard?
Church is a structured home base.
Church is amazing and full with grace.
Church brings the words of our Father.
Church isn't annoying, never a bother.
Church yields fruit on which we can feast.
Church is the place where we beat the beast.
Church is mighty; give us more.
Church is where a choir can soar.
Church brings us down on our knees.
Church has the ability to always go please.
In church, we bring out our Sunday best.

Church is working above all the rest.

Church leaves the worried feeling complete.

Church is really quite unique.

Church makes us give praise to the Father.

Church can be loud with joyful hollers.

Church has many pews to be filled.

Church is something we steadily build.

Churches are found in cities and forests.

Church can be filled with the rich and the poorest.

Church is where GOoD news gets delivered to the masses.

Church is where we find rainbows through the stained glasses.

Rainbows live together in colors.

Nothing says God loves you like a double rainbow.

Rainbows are God's covenant, a promise of love.

"And the bow shall be in the cloud; and I will look upon it, that I may remember the everlasting covenant between God and every living creature of all flesh that is upon the earth" (Genesis 9:16).

Bring in some cheer and harvest good fortune.

Breathe in the air, a testimony of God's love.

Before the rush, fires of love.

There once was a path; they called it Old Broadway.

Keep on seeking, and you will keep on finding.

Tranquility exists in places found holy.

Praise to the Holy Ghost for all His efforts. He is the hard worker.

Keep pressing along like a sloth's doggie paddle.

These two words can lead you to greatness: gentle love.

You must keep faith alive when there is none, you must keep hope alive when there is none, and you must keep love alive when there is none.

Proverbs

Honesty is always the best route for good love.

It's never too late to say you're sorry.

Wisdom can never be spoken with half a heart.

Grab a hold of stability and hang on it for dear life.

Try to nurture a clean conscious like a deer nurses her young.

Stay away from all-night snake parties.

There is nothing worse than manifesting snakes on a spiritual level.

It takes time and forgiveness to heal all wounds.

If you can't please yourself, how do you expect to please others?

There's nothing a big bear hug can't solve.

When receiving money for a service you did, it's okay to be polite and say no three times to it, but on the fourth time, it's legal for you to take it without feeling guilty.

Always have clean socks and shoes that don't smell; once a shoe goes sour, it ruins everything in your demeanor.

It's polite to take off your shoes when entering someone's house.

Holding your lover's hand when you go on long walks is a sign of great affection and will ultimately keep you young at heart.

Keep the Lord's wishes in mind in all things you do.

If there is something that isn't quite right, bring it to the surface and reconnect with it. A peaceful solution must be found once again in order to move on with life.

If someone has peace, it's better not to break it with an old folly. Hold your tongue and avoid destruction once again.

It's best to hold a conversation voice to voice; there's only so much a text message can convey.

It's okay to judge yourselves, for this will lead you to proper correction.

Hold the innocence of a child and try to play while you work.

Stay young at heart.

There are many special things hidden in caverns below the earth.

Don't dig your own grave early. Stay away from magic that will continually backfire against you time and time again.

The freaks come out at night and plot mischief during the day.

If you're a freak, it's almost impossible to be a good lover. Ditch the freak in Freakville.

Don't be bitter when you don't get your way; the problem is usually because you were off with something in the first place.

New Year's Day is always the best day of the year to make art. As an artist, you must work hard on this day.

The first snowfall of the year is usually one of the strongest days to make art. Do only holy and positive ventures on this day.

Your Father in heaven wants to make art with you. He wants to see what you can do for Him and what you can do together as well.

Have you ever seen a ventriloquist with a dummy? That's you when you do too much drugs.

If you can't reach someone after a lengthy, reasonable discussion of religion, then just brush the dirt off your sneakers and move on to the next person.

Growing spiritually is just like getting your hair cut; you cut off the bad and unmanageable hair and save the rest to be reshaped and reworked.

You can't please everyone all the time; don't let it get to you. Do what you can, and rejoice in it.

Sometimes, you just need silence, like closing the TV before bedtime to read the Bible.

Try not to sleep with the TV on while you sleep because it will influence and corrupt your dreams. Bet on that.

A lie compounds your life like an interest in a debt.

Proverbs

To properly evaluate the correct amount of time for each task at hand is a good skill to have.

Faith is like throwing darts blindfolded and hitting the target.

You can do anything once you raise your inner frequency levels.

Positive things attract positive things.

Having a sober mind helps in all your dealings.

Never be blindsided by fortune and fame; always stay humble in all of your works.

It is honorable to sit in the sun.

There is no need to be so known.

You better hope you can balance the scale.

Get on the offense; manifest some good love.

There's no defense like a good offense.

Religion is like a game of chess; you have to think far ahead in order to win.

Religion is like chess; it's a game of black versus white.

Sometimes, we must crash and burn before we rise from the ashes.

Keep your faith no matter what is said against you. You must have faith in order to conquer the hate.

The hater prays for your downfall, while the lover prays for good fortune.

Steady rise to the dawn of a positive light, fight the good fight for life.

It's almost impossible to put trust and faith into faceless voices, but in some voices, you can place all your trust.

Drinks are always served for the toast of the town.

Half the battle is getting the correct information.

Keep your focus on positive reinforcement.

Whenever you break something, it becomes twenty more beautiful things.

If you find the face of adversity, you have found where your work lies.

Faith is like an eagle falling in mating.

It's up to you to keep love alive.

Magic and cheap tricks hold no real power.

There are many different realms and realities one can open up; make sure you stay on the right playing field. The devil has many tricks and realms to keep you in a state of temptation. Be aware of your surroundings and the keeper of them.

When making wishes or wants, keep it simple so that they always come true. Don't get greedy.

When the chips are down, and everything seems to come out wrong, you still must have faith in the Lord.

A fool is always sad, but a wise man is constantly happy.

Become the impossible no matter the odds against you.

You must fight for your rights because you're human.

Lift up your love and let the rest stay buried in the rebuking graveyard.

Don't get derailed by ill thoughts, but find the right positive thoughts that will get you to heaven.

Sometimes, there's nothing you can do but leave it in God's hands.

There is no trying to balance the scale; you're either good or bad.

Let love be the dominating force in your life.

Paying tribute and giving back is essential for spiritual growth and proper respect.

Don't focus on negative things because you might get stuck in regret; focus on the lighter side of things and free your mind from past failures. Live and let it go, let it go, let it go, go, go.

Proverbs

Spiritual rebirth and regeneration are essential for positive growth. These usually come after long nights of awakenings and self-discoveries. Then you are a baby again. Knowing everything and nothing at the same time. You become reborn.

Don't put words in unfinished sentences.

Sometimes, thinking fast will be the death of you. Slow your thoughts, and you will succeed.

Things were decided upon before you were even born. God has a plan for everything.

God gives us free will; it's up to us to manifest the correct path.

Being kind and always gentle will bring you to new heights.

To make art is a gift from God; create with understanding. Even your bad ones are good.

Carry the burden for those who can't.

At the core of an apple, good prevails.

It may take a long time to find your place, but you'll know when it's right. You'll feel the presence of a higher authority working within you, and you'll know it's the right move.

When opportunity presents itself, seize it with quickness before you lose that blessing.

There is much to learn from a turtle's slowness.

It's always a joyous occasion when spotting an albino deer.

Even crocodiles are peaceful when they have full bellies.

"If thine enemy be hungry, give him bread to eat; and if he be thirsty, give him water to drink: For thou shalt heap coals of fire upon his head, and the Lord shall reward thee" (Proverbs 25:21–22).

The wages of war can be costly, but it may hold honor in the end.

When at war, you must know when to strike when the iron's hot, and when you do, be ruthless at it like a lion hunting its prey.

"A time to rend, and a time to sew; a time to keep silence, and a time to speak; A time to love, and a time to hate; a time of war, and a time of peace" (Ecclesiastes 3:7–8).

The war in Ukraine can be stopped if only they would share a bottle of vodka with the Russians.

If you focus all your efforts on war, then war will find you.

Make hugs, not bombs.

You know if you're doing good when you hear the whispers of your grandparents' joy.

Try to please the angels in heaven with all your actions.

Think, "Would Jesus do this?" Before you do something stupid.

"Thou shalt not commit adultery" (Exodus 20:14). This is one of the Ten Commandments.

Once you're on the God algorithm, there's no turning back. Nothing but loves, and likes, and prayers, and Scripture, and amen.

When you're stuck in a corner, paint another corner.

Never be ashamed to have a family.

Don't forget the importance of Father's Day; you have a Father in heaven who loves you very much too.

Evil can't do a thing when love and light are shining.

You must be strong, like the mighty buffalo.

It's good to set reminders so that you know where you came from.

No animal can take the fish away from the eagle.

Birds nest in the trees and rocks of the friendly.

A cat's tail is a radar for love.

Never let a stranger determine your entire fate.

Sometimes, you must take risks for the things you love.

Love comes in many forms, but gentle love is the best.

When you find happiness, hold onto it, and don't let anyone take it away from you.

Some people are just focused on hate and fail to see potential in the situations at hand.

Just love and let love, and it will find you.

Constantly be the seeker of wisdom and ask God for her beauty.

When you hear something so many times, you're almost forced to believe it. Seek the truth in all situations. Don't believe the hype, especially if it's served on a cold dish.

Win the Lord's favor, and you shall be happy.

Trust is earned and not given, so do your best to make things right when trying to obtain love and affection from a mentor or teacher.

To craft the "art of love" is one of the greatest challenges as an artist but one of the most rewarding when your seeds grow in full bloom and your art comes alive.

When you speak words of wisdom, they must be spoken with total confidence and authority.

To be a king is a great honor but a heavy burden for he who wears the crown. Wisdom must rule his judgments, and they must always be in accordance with God's laws of righteousness.

The wicked will stop at nothing to try and get payback for the lack of love and their non-understanding of things. They'd rather do something evil and sin more than admit defeat or even try to understand the correct way. They're just wicked by nature.

The wicked does not accept the love of Jesus and will perish for it.

People who worship Satan think that they are a religion, but the truth is that they are the antireligion, and no government can protect them from God's judgment, which is the ultimate law.

What's fair is fair, and what's not fair are the lies of the devil and his followers, who plot wickedness at every instant.

The devil knows your dirt and your weaknesses, and he will always exploit them on the ones you love in order to separate you from good love or from obtaining happiness. So beware of sins left uncovered.

If you deserve shame and an unruly judgment of character, then you must own up to your failures in order to pay back for what you did. And you can't complain either because you did it to yourself.

Mercy is a tool of the wise, but there's only so much one can take before effective action must be taken place and justice is sought as a solution to the problem.

Always try to forgive the one who hurt you. Without forgiveness, you can never heal properly.

Take time with a gentle heart and tend to its loving affections.

The Holy Ghost is the hardest worker in the game; always give praise to His honor.

You must believe it to achieve it, and super faith is the solution.

It doesn't matter what you do; as long as you're true to God and his laws, then everything will be okay.

Without permission, you can't do anything. Always ask for the rights to do something spiritual.

You can't be spiritual without the love of God or knowledge thereof.

It is impossible to argue with angry, faceless critics; avoid their path to madness and sadness.

Always have time to give your full love and full affection.

It's always the right time for love and affection.

The more faith you have in God and Jesus, the happier your life will become.

Sometimes, you realize you've been wrong and lied to for years, and it hurts. You must take this burning fire and mold it and put it around a rock to help tame it again and then make it your new foundation for future strength. Never let a fire rage uncontrollably.

Who can escape an angry lion or a hungry tiger?

Who can escape a king's wrath when injustice is done?

After you finish dancing, it is proper for a sweetheart to bring you some water.

Dancing together can be one of the greatest blessings in the world that God can grant.

Words are for fools, but the wise hold their tongue.

Be careful not to isolate yourself for hours alone; it could lead to vain, clouded judgment. Always get fresh air and try to reconnect with a family member or loved one for relief and a fresh perspective on things.

The God we serve is always fair in His judgments; He is very patient when it comes to right and wrong dealings.

It is possible to coexist with a lover here on earth and in the spirit realm as well. We are both connected, and we can spread our energies in both places at the same time. Some on earth and some in the spirit world. This is an example of what happens when loved ones who have crossed come seek us for some reason for healing or enlightenment, either in a dream or in real life, with a force of some profound connection. It is possible to have split energies.

Love must be patient and enduring and have a willingness to overlook flaws and defects of character. You must love even when they don't have any to give you at that time. Then you know that your love is true.

In order to love properly, you must give your full trust to your lover. Without trust, you have nothing.

Your lover must be willing to admit their wrongdoings when they happen. If they can't see their unjust loving actions and refuse to give in when a wrong was done, then it's not true love, and you should leave the situation before you get even more hurt. But remember to always have forgiveness in your true love tool belt. That will bring you to new heights.

When you love someone, and you can't stay apart from them, maybe it's a sign that love exists here, and it should be nurtured at all costs.

If someone doesn't feel right anymore, delete them from your existence. It wasn't meant to be, but if there's the tiniest of sparks that are still there, then help kindle the fire back to full passion. There is more to gain and learn from by reconnecting and putting forth your best effort to save and cherish a relationship.

When your emotions run wild, tame them with wisdom.

Money will ruin just about every relationship you have in one way or another. Try to rise above its roots of slavery and be free of its confines.

An eagle will fly higher than the storm cloud and avoid dangerous situations.

If only we knew the names of our guardian angels and guides, wouldn't life be easier?

Sometimes, God tests the strength of a man's character. He will bring conflict in order to build courage and faith.

To go against your parents' wishes is foolish.

"Honour thy father and thy mother: that thy days may be long upon the land which the Lord thy God giveth thee" (Exodus 20:12). The Ten Commandments.

God gives you many paths to choose from, so choose wisely. Some may lead to destruction.

When the enemy presents itself to you, you must have no fear and have the heart of a rock to overcome all obstacles and threats that are going to come your way.

Don't dwell in regret; it can swallow a man whole. Just push forward like a diamond dove flying across the ever-changing sky.

When staring the impossible in the face, burn your laser eye beams right through it.

When they say you're no good and you're bound for failure, that's when you must try even harder. We must fight for the things we love. Nothing comes easy.

Living on the wire can get drastic at times, but years of battles should prepare you for anything challenging.

The word n***** is a curse word for all who use it, and it only brings hate and destruction.

Sometimes, you're the only one who knows the correct answer, and if you don't share it with those around you, it will become your enslavement.

If the bad begins to outweigh the good, you have to dead it before it deads you.

"Watch out for them dead ends. You never know which way you're heading if you don't know where you're going" (Henry Cook).

Give joy and constant praise to the Lord, for He deserves it.

Keep your wits in all that you do; don't fall victim to new wine.

"The fear of the Lord is the beginning of wisdom: and the knowledge of the holy is understanding" (Proverbs 9:10).

Believe in the power of love and what it can concur if you have it in your heart, mind, and soul.

Sometimes, there is nothing that can change your mind about a certain issue except a catalytic softness in the heart.

Praying without ceasing is the way of the wise.

Only fools drink satanic tea.

Love must be patient in order to percolate.

Nothing in life is that easy; there's always the hard road of doing things.

When you fight for your love, you will be tested many times along the way.

There's no such thing as an easy process except easy loving.

When God gives you room to breathe, say thank you.

Never pick a fight with the devil unless you're willing to go all the way.

Bring peace and prosperity to your church picnic.

Money is the greatest obstacle of our century.

Money brings out the worst in people. Don't let it own your soul.

If it was meant to be, then God put His blessing on it; if it wasn't meant to be, you're up a creek without a paddle, but there's always hope. God can change anything if it's your time.

When you find a lover who is worthy, fight for their honor and don't hold back.

When you find true love, your darkest nights turn to light.

When your lover jeopardizes your entire relationship over a simple lust for someone other than you, you better have forgiveness in your heart if you want it to survive. And know how to apply it correctly too.

When you're in a relationship you're going to feel cheated in some fashion at some point in one way or another. It's how you recover from it that determines the size of your love and love that is to be.

Go to great depths for the sake of love and its gentleness.

To become a great lover, you must become super empathic to your lover's needs and wants at all times.

Don't carry the mistakes of your past relationships into your new lover's presence. It's time to love properly like a normal human being in love without mistakes and the same old regrets again.

Leave the pimp at home in the dirt where he belongs when attempting to articulate a new lover. The pimp will tear the concepts of good love apart. His motives are greedy and selfish.

Lying is so unattractive and destructive that most choose to deny it when it happens right in front of their face.

Even the simplest of things can be a blessing in disguise.

We cannot just depend on ourselves to self-sustain; we need the love of others to survive.

When faced with major affliction and atrocities it is important to take and live one breath at a time. If you can survive one breath, then you can make the next one, and then to the next till slowly, you start to breathe and maneuver again like a normal human being.

Do not let time capture the best of you; patience comes with wisdom.

A fool will replay his foolishness on repeat for the world to see, but the wise knows how to silence and hold his thoughts.

Sometimes, we take risks beyond our comfort zone in hopes of high reward, and sometimes, a fool chooses to go broke by his own handle.

Please remember you're not alone even when you think you're alone. There's always someone there watching and waiting over you in heaven.

Sometimes, our destinies are planned before us, and sometimes, we plan our destiny.

It is important to remember that God holds all the keys that you need to open the doors to your life.

Remember to give proper time to the Lord each and every day.

How many are worthy to command the angels in a time of war?

In times of danger, you must keep your cool like Fonzi; "aaaaaa aaaaaaaaaaaaaaaaaaaaaaa!"

There is nothing worse than a guilty mind to hold your shame hostage; this is what demons feed off of.

People should not crush one another's hopes or dreams but let them dream and let them hope as long as they can. Don't be a dream crusher.

Sometimes, you can wait days for an answer from God on a subject, and that's okay.

Direct your ways around raising a child, and you shall learn some of life's most sacred blessings.

An eagle mates when he finds his equal lover. Then they dive.

Love is watching an elephant paint a portrait.

Every ship shall sail a rough sea once in its lifetime.

Use passionate words and prose when courting a woman who's fair.

Sometimes, half the battle is knowing who the enemy is. The devil has many disguises.

Keep the Lord your God close to your heart and in all that you do.

Words of true affection are usually accompanied by soft tears.

Mold the world into your dreamiest dream possible and let the fruits of the subconscious ooze unto the awakened state of mind that rules the day.

Truths and lies are both found in the sleepless states of mind.

Truths cannot be escaped when it's time for the Holy Ghost live wire.

"Thou shalt not steal" (Exodus 20:15). This is one of the Ten Commandments.

A state of war can be exhausting, so don't start a fight you can't

Proverbs

finish properly.

When it's a season for love, none can do you no wrong, and none shall bring in the hate. Love just loves and cannot be tampered with.

Loving is the season. Have some faith now. God will save us.

You can say whatever you like to me, but it's the Lord's authority whom you have to win the favor of.

Jesus wept while He rode the donkey into Jerusalem.

There are only so many threats one man can take before he starts to lose hope. O how horrible this is.

Blessed is he who tells the truth even when he is trying to hide.

A king can fly as high as an eagle but can fall just as fast.

Don't let the simple words that fade away be renewed by subjective thoughts of continuing reprimanding insubordination.

Just when you think you're done, you realize you're not even close to being finished.

Even a little lie can ruin months of love and affection.

There is nothing worse than not living up to your spiritual potential.

Even the Lord directs the path of lightning.

It's better to not know than to know and still rebel.

Keep your mind and actions rooted in peacefulness and surrounded by joy at all times.

Joy can be found in an abundance of churches.

Write a poem of affection to your lover and declare it to the airs abroad for good manifestation.

Danger follows those who are deemed wicked.

I haven't seen God lose yet, so why do you still choose wickedness? If you do, you've lost, and you don't even know it.

Don't let bitterness deter you from greatness; curb your emotions.

You can replace the negative words that hurt your soul with positive words in your trigger state of speaking. For example, tell yourself that every time you're going to think of the word "b****," replace it with "itch" instead at the root of its manifestation. So next time, you just say "itch" from the start, which is a lot better than saying "b****" all the time. Practice this, and soon, you will be free from all negative words and only speaking positive things.

There is nothing worse than obtaining a bad reputation; try to avoid this at all costs.

Keep your distance from men who are destructive by nature.

To say someone's going to jail is to put a curse upon them.

Demons love to spit.

When you read the Bible, your eye vision improves and adapts.

Be careful when dolls are in the hands of the wicked.

Enjoy the silence.

The devil should always be under your heel where he belongs.

It's possible to make it rain in the valley of death; o how joyful it is!

Forgive, or else you won't be forgiven.

"I will bless the Lord at all times: his praise shall continually be in my mouth" (Psalm 34:1).

Put God first above all family.

When all your friends and family tell you that something is bad for you, you better listen up and respect their advice.

A wise man knows how to please his family and friends without fret or fuss.

Don't let temptation lead you toward fast rewards.

Sometimes, you must let people go, even if your heart says to connect. Reason says let go.

There is no use in moaning over spilled milk; get a sponge and clean it up.

Sometimes, you can be on top of the world and then a second later become under the earth. That's just life with religion sometimes.

You can tell a man's worth by the fruits that he bears.

If everywhere you go there is destruction and chaos, you must change your ways before it's too late.

A fool will fall in love with the wrong woman over and over again.

You can't always get what you want; it's a fact of life.

Be cautious of strange women who come lurking in the middle of the night. Their words may be soothing, but their intentions are poisonous.

Doing drugs lowers your morals and expectations; you need to think clear-headed when dealing with religious beliefs.

A junkie can always tell you a good story to learn from.

Sometimes folding is your only option, so fold.

God answers prayers in His way, not yours.

Be careful when using a man's name; you don't want to hold him accountable for something he didn't do.

Don't ever get caught with your pants down; it only leads to your own disgrace and embarrassment.

A junkie's ways are based on foolishness and selfishness.

Don't be fooled or blinded by promises of easy riches; nothing in this world comes easy or is for free but God's love.

Never underestimate the willingness to deceit by the mouth of a thief. They will even lie on a stack of Bibles if they must. They have no spine or empathy in their soul.

The soul is ruled by destiny. What's yours?

To deliver justice is a serious act. It takes honor, courage, and a super faith.

God determines who shall hear this or that, and there is purpose in His choices. So, feel blessed if you hear a whispering word from a holy stranger and feel blessed if you hear the bitterness of the enemy. Each is a blessing from God.

Lessons can be learned whenever we come full circle to return to a prior situation of concern.

The fool will live in a state of wanting, and the righteous shall be satisfied with what is.

If you want to learn something special, give all your money to the poor and follow Jesus.

Don't be roped in by lavish displays of material wealth; they come rooted in vanity and greed.

Never make fun of the rich man in his castle; you don't know what he did to deserve what he has. He may just be blessed by God.

Never make fun of the poor man in his dwellings; you don't know what he did that got him in that position in the first place. It's wrong to judge.

Most rich men will not inherit the kingdom of heaven.

If a thief wants something so badly, just give it to him and then pray for his salvation. He'll get his in the end.

You must rule your kingdom with mercy, but God makes a time for justice too.

Writing something down in writing puts a holy seal to it and helps it to manifest.

It's all about holding four-dimensional visions in a one-dimensional world.

Your future should never be trusted to a deck of tarot cards. There is no logic in them, only chance and speculation.

Remember to thank God for all of the little things that add up to making a big thing.

One can only learn from a repeated process of failures.

The goal is to fashion correctly the first time and have the correct first choices you make when doing something creative. To do this is a blessing from God.

A fool won't listen to advice from his friends and family.

A son or daughter who leads their family into shame is not worth anything.

All the security passwords in the world can't stop the power of love.

Many people fall into temptation because they are poor in spirit.

Don't let dollar signs control your emotions and decisions.

If you don't like what you see in the mirror, then change it.

Your inner thoughts can't be hidden by your chemical makeup.

There are over 5,360 blessings that one can receive; try to get them all.

Only a few get to see the face of the Lord, but His spirit is everywhere in anything and everything.

Say, "There'll be none of that," when there should be no evil to be had.

Long to connect with the Lord day and night without ceasing.

Special treatment and privileges should be given to all women who are breastfeeding. This is a delicate and crucial act that should be respected.

It's never too late to say you're sorry.

Some things are better left unsaid and not cause any more harm than what's already taken place.

If you want forgiveness, you must hold it in your heart toward others, or else the Lord will not hear you.

The pathway to heaven cannot be bought.

Give quality time to those who need some special help of some sort.

You'd be amazed at what the spirit can do when it's raised to the occasion.

Reading the Bible to one another is a sign of great affection.

The Book of Enoch fills you in on the secret thoughts of the Holy One and offers a slightly different take than the writings in the Bible. It's a must-read.

When you're in the flow, don't stop until you can go no more. Give it your all when you're blessed with the act of creation. The payoff is usually grand.

We were formed in God's image, and man can pack a mighty spiritual punch in the psychical and non-visible realms as well, depending upon how high our spiritual energy level is.

Praying is the greatest invention of the universe.

You can't be worried about failure and not being worthy all the time; it's not healthy for the soul. Instead, say and think that you are worthy to begin with, and success will follow.

Nobody was perfect, but Jesus was flawless.

The stories in the Bible are like a good basket of fresh fruits.

Take your time when it comes to love, for one of the principles of love must be based on patience.

In a world full of broad ways, take the narrow path.

The sun sustains all life; the world grows and needs the warmth of its fire to survive.

When trouble befalls you, and you slip into sinful ways, just remember God will always give you a choice to help get you out. His mercies are great, but it's up to you to make the right decision to get out at that proper time. For if you don't, there will surely be fire and disillusion in your path for the rest of that day and night.

With the rising of the sun comes a renewal of life and spirit on earth. This brings a new chance and a good starting point in which to make things right again and regain favor with the Lord.

When walking somewhere, don't drag your feet; that's a sign of laziness.

Stand at attention when the authority is speaking.

Leave all bitterness and resentment shut and buried in the rebuking graveyard.

Follow your dreams till the bitter ends of this earth and never stop trying to manifest their greatness.

It is healthy to spend at least two hours a day connecting to the Lord somehow.

Begin and end each day with prayers to your Father in heaven.

Never forget to include the animals and Mother Earth in your daily prayers.

Making time to love your lover correctly is like creating a fine piece of art that will always shine.

Children hold some keys to salvation.

A child's dreams should not go unnoticed or passed over, for there is sacred meaning in them all.

There is nothing that spells out love like a full house of chattering family.

Everything in the world is exactly where it is supposed to be, and it's always the right time.

Don't mistake kindness for weakness, for kindness is a tool of the brave.

There's nothing worse in the world than wasted talent.

A standing bear can sometimes lash out.

Nothing in the world spells out joy like a tiny polar bear playing in the snow with its siblings.

Sometimes, you can get the church giggles, which is joyful and disrespectful at the same time. Beware of the church giggles; they're just plain silly.

There is nothing like hearing a sermon of fire from a blessed preacher.

A pastor's work is never done, and he is always required to be on the wire twenty-four seven.

Which came first, the chicken or the rock? Rock!

Rejoice in the days that the Lord makes for us; sing a song of praise in His honor.

Cry, cry, cry, cry, and shout until the sun falls down. Then there will be no more time for tears.

"Thou shalt not take the name of the Lord thy God in vain; for the Lord will not hold him guiltless that taketh his name in vain" (Exodus 20:7). This is one of the Ten Commandments.

Reading the Bible is like jumping rope with perfect timing. Give it your all until you miss a skip, then try again. Get into the rhythm.

Techno music can bring you to a higher state of consciousness.

A wartime minister must also be a master at finding peace.

Super faith is a level of righteousness in the heart and can be obtained by anyone who cares enough to put their trust into the Lord greatly with all their heart and soul.

Hope can never die; it can only be grown if you have spiritual intentions.

Love is a tiny bear rolling down a steep incline.

Love is letting someone skip into line.

Love can be found even in Blacklights.

Love can usually end all fights.

Love is a text that says goodnight.

Love is on the horizon; it's always in sight.

Love is a voice to put to a face.

Proverbs

Love is the force to put you in place.
Love is surrounding you everywhere in a church.
Love is the bark peeling from a birch.
Love is watching the Berlin Wall fall.
Love is a giraffe standing tall.
Love is waking up early to wake someone up early.
Love is living in a world not worldly.
Love is a kiss before bedtime.
Love is glowing; it always shines.
Love is being corrected by your father.
Love is a walk with your father.
Love is seen in a mourning dove on the ground.
Love for the city and walking around.
Love is driving slowly to avoid killing deer.
Love conquers all, even the fear.
Love is cherishing personal items of the deceased.
Love is a family having a big feast.
Love is a visit to a loved one in a hospital bed.
Love is praying to the Lord, shaking in your bed.
Love is Indian lovers walking at sunset.
Love for the eagle that flies like a jet.
Love is dancing with your sweetheart.
Love connects; don't tear it apart.
Love is letting your dog lick your mouth.
Love are the birds migrating south.
Love is telling stories around a campfire.
Love is the correction that comes from the wire.
Love is reuniting with a long-lost friend.
Love picks up and always will bend.
Love is your best-case scenario syndrome.

Love is a dog getting meat from a bone.
Love is finding the king in kings cake.
Love is the baking of a kings cake.
Love is a dancing Indian covered in sweat.
Love for the whales that always stay wet.
Love is bringing water to your sweetheart.
Love is the making of sacred soft art.
Love is reconnecting with lost items in a dream.
Love is a kiss under a moonbeam.
Love is a golden green freedom field.
Love for the vineyard and what it shall yield.
Love is a good reputation.
Love can direct a nation.
Love is patient; love is kind.
Love is always top of mind.
Love is making the A-team.
Love is a godsent, powerful dream.
Love is the reward of your artistic endeavors.
Love for the fox, so sly and so clever.
Love is a random compliment.
Love's divine and heaven-sent.
Love is an extra enduring smile.
Love is walking that extra mile.
Love is time when you've thrust.
Love is clean; it never gets dusted.
Love is gentle and so kind.
Love is ours, yours and mine.
Love is writing some love words.
Love is helping wounded, broken birds.
Love is a soothing singing song.

Proverbs

Love holds you tight all day long.
Love is a laugh, two or three.
Love is happy super with glee.
Love is sharing all of my breakfast.
Love is supporting like a broken leg cast.
Love is a romantic dinner.
Love is always grown by winners.
Love is kissing on top of the Empire State.
Love is staying on the phone with your lover up late.
Love is consuming like fire.
Love is the words sung by a choir.
Love is your burning desire.
Love is water that puts off fires.
Love is more soothing than any pill.
Love can change the fate of the ill.
Love is saying, "God bless you."
Love is better when there are two.
Love is finding some new shoes.
Love for the black and for the blues.
Love is a prayer from a stranger.
Love will keep you away from danger.
Love is alive and still kicking.
Loves together constantly sticking.
Love is floating on the lazy river.
Love's a blanket that stops you from the shivers.
Love is giving your last bite away.
Love will always save the day.
Love is for the first responders.
Loves for stoics and all their ponders.
Love for all the sleepy doctors.

Love for all the wild punk rockers.
Love for Big Bird and the thunder.
Love for the octopuses deep down under.
Love is for the uniformed choir.
Love is held at a funeral pier.
Love for all of the children.
A gentle love will always win.
Love for Jesus and His works.
Love for haters and jerks.
Love for the man in all black.
Love when the good guys attack.
Love for the church we must build.
Love for the deers that they killed.
Love for gummy worms and bears.
Love for the eagle who go dares.
Love for the efforts that you gave.
Love for Elijah in the cave.
Love goes with you burning bright.
Love comes from soft candle lights.
Love shows you a better way.
Love for the flowers that bloom in May.
Love can cure the deaf and blind.
Love can be transmitted from your mind.
Love can find a Kicking Bird.
Love's the answer, haven't you heard?
Love for brothers working it out.
Love for hyenas who love to shout.
Love is big, bold, and bright.
Love is quite an amazing sight.
Love is grandparents who sneak in a kiss.

Love can be fruitful, tender, and bliss.
Love brings forth good intentions.
Love to the winners and the honorable mentions.
Love for the seagull stealing French fries.
Love is magnetic through one's eyes.
Love for ducks wearing pink hats.
Love for the bats, cats, and the rats.
Love sounds great in drums of the ears.
Love will always conquer all fears.
Love for when the Eiffel Tower flashes.
Love for the boxer named Clay Cassius.
Love is welcoming, like a smile.
Love is for the argyle bathroom title.
Love is always kept in style.
Love is to keep always on file.
Love for 911 and angels.
Love for all the guardian angels.
Love plays a game full of trust.
Love is something that can't go bust.
Deliverance can only work for the self-willing.

There must be constant communication for love to fly between lovers. Communication is key.

Don't let the devil tempt you with promises of riches and a quick family.

There comes a point where you can't be stepped on no more and you step on the foot that's trying to step on you.

If someone can't talk to you over the phone and they want to text all the time, you know that that relationship is a fougasse. Human voice-to-voice interaction is necessary for a healthy relationship.

If you think you're in love with a person and they don't say good morning or goodnight to you at the beginning and end of each day, then they're worthless.

Don't be too eager when falling into a romance; your desperation will be taken advantage of. Harvest your inner romantic turtle. Take your time. Love is patient.

If a text says one hundred words, FaceTiming says a million.

Don't be blinded by dollar signs. They can only lead you to vanity and greed.

Greed can destroy a man's reputation with quickness.

"Thou shalt have no other gods before me" (Exodus 20:3). This is one of the Ten Commandments

Be slow to anger in all situations; don't jump to rash judgments.

Give it enough time, and the truth will always emerge. It always does. Always!

Joy can be found by watching a doggie dream while they take a nap on your bed lying next to you.

Always be ready to go to the extreme at any time, day or night. Take it to the limit, and don't look back.

When you see a red flag, respect it for what it brings: danger and another red flag. Call it quits before you get too many of them. If you don't listen, you'll just be a fool with a bunch of red flags, living with multiple regrets.

It is nice to have family; pay attention when they are giving you advice.

Be wary of someone who says they don't like animals.

Wisdom comes in many forms; one of them is celibacy.

Mass looting is demonic behavior, as well as starting fires in protests. These are two behaviors they do in hell.

A liar will eventually get caught in his own lies. It's only a matter of time before he slips.

Proverbs

A wise man sometimes plays a fool to catch one.

Only God is allowed to break your heart.

When reading the Bible, it's good to keep a dictionary close by so that you can look up all the words you don't understand.

Each story of the Bible has its own flavor, just like the menu on the side of an ice-cream truck.

It's important to read all types of scriptures. Being well-rounded in all religions leads to wisdom.

Try and be a love pleaser and submit to your partner's wants and needs.

Do all you can to avoid a fight. If someone's negative, settle it by being happy and choosing positivity.

If a person avoids a question, they are usually hiding something they're embarrassed about or they don't understand yet.

Dreamers are builders and are responsible for shaping the future of all things.

Never fart while in church. Go outside if you must, or use the bathroom. Be polite and respectful.

There is a spirit in the dawn of morning that trumps all other times of day.

No words of wisdom can be found in the heart of a liar.

Once you've cheated on your lover, you might as well call it quits because the love is gone from that very moment.

God is eagerly waiting for you to live up to your full spiritual potential.

Be happy with the simple things; it creates more joy in your life.

The paths to heaven are skinny and narrow. Most fall off.

To join the A-team, you must bring you're A-game consistently.

You must earn the armor of God and the right to put it on.

A shield of faith is awarded to those who have expressed extreme courage in times of adversity.

When a king is crowned king, he must use righteousness to keep it and make it worthy to be worn.

Temporary setbacks are a part of the spiritual process; there is much to learn from setbacks. Sometimes, a setback can be a setup.

It is important to surrender to God at the beginning of every new day; it keeps you on track.

You can never pray too much, for prayer is the great connector to our Lord.

Make sure that every minute of your day is devoted to a higher purpose; time is but so fleeting.

When you have God in the brain, who can get Him off it?

The words "God's got me" should always be an honor.

When you think the work is done, you are usually not done; there is always more room to sacrifice your efforts.

As much as God appreciates hard work, He also wants us to rest up and not work so hard all the time.

Hold love close to your heart, and don't let the haters tarnish it.

What God declares is written, and it cannot be altered; his judgments are definite.

Paying tribute is always a good thing, but actions speak louder than words.

Do all you can to help your brother or neighbor, and do it with joy in your heart, not bitterness.

It is possible to have two separate thoughts coming from each side of the brain at the same time.

Transgender people are humans, too, and deserve just as much love as any others. God loves us all.

Be careful not to spoil a good deed with a filthy thought in between.

Proverbs

What you think matters just as much as what you speak and show. All your thoughts are read by angels and written on your heart to see as well.

Devoting at least two hours a day to the Lord is a healthy habit.

Never stop giving praise to the Lord. He deserves it.

Even aliens agree that Jesus was a real person.

Heaven isn't too far away if you're living for it.

Treat your spouse like the king or queen she is. Treat them better than a pound of rubies.

"Lead us not into temptation" is a good law to rule the flesh by.

"Deliver us from evil" are great words to live by and should be practiced at all costs.

To be a good lover, one must first mend several broken hearts.

Jesus is not happy that they turned Christmas into a heavy, jolly man who owns sweatshops in the North Pole and who decides who's been naughty or nice and to give you coal or presents.

The lower spiritual realms are still ruled by God and His authority.

God will test your faith at least once or twice a day. Will you pass?

Devil worship comes in many forms; most don't even know when they are doing it.

There is no balance between good and evil; there is either up or down; which way are you heading?

Try to make things right by God; repent from your heart and soul to make amends for your sins.

The way of the sinner is covered in filth, and he awaits an unruly death.

Remember, it's not just this life you have to worry about, but where you go when you die is just as important.

It's hard not to be worried all the time when you are surrounded by death and fire. Change your ways.

God already knows what you need before you even ask it.

It's important to write things down. In heaven, they record everything, and there are hundreds of holy books written by angels like Metatron.

Fallen angels become demons for eternity.

Live your life free from worry; God wants you to be happy and prosper.

What happens to one person in the Bible can happen to you, too, so count your blessings and receive the Lord's covenants.

Preach the good news whenever and wherever you can; this is your Christian duty.

Make sure what you speak of is correct information; there is nothing worse than spitting lies.

A fool can never give good advice to help someone out of a situation.

Sometimes, we are so blinded by beauty that we fail to see the ugly truths about a certain person.

A malicious woman will use beauty to blind her prey.

Even the appearance of money can be spiritually destructive. Don't get trapped with dollar signs in your eyes.

Don't get your hopes up that strange women will bring you happiness, even if they are fair to look at. They may talk a sly game, but they are still strange.

Faith and love cannot be found in any AI.

When a turtle falls in love, he is patient and slow.

Disease may follow in the ways of a sinner.

Save yourself the trouble, suppress your desires from the jump and avoid the suffering.

Proverbs

You should start every meal with a thoughtful prayer of thanksgiving.

You need not worry because God already knows your situation.

If you pray for a blessing and believe that you will receive it, then you will receive it.

What God does for one person can happen to you too.

Spiritual gifts are gifts that cannot be taken back or lost, no matter what your situation is or becomes.

In heaven, there are beautiful dragons that fly across the clouds.

When you see a red flag in someone's behavior, that means stop and go no further; save yourself the trouble.

Keeping faith is like walking over a minefield blindfolded.

Lovers may come and go, but a good friend lasts forever, and his worth holds great weight.

It's not that you have special needs as a lover; it's that you know better and expect only the best treatment from them that you deserve.

In a world that's full of madness, one must exercise gladness and gratitude and endless amounts of joy.

They won't take you seriously if they don't see good fruits from your pickings.

Having the faith of a mustard seed can bring you into the miracle realm.

Most miracles don't happen without extreme sacrifice.

Fasting is a weapon of the brave and determined.

Learn to hold your fire in stillness. Be a steady flame of power.

Which came first, the chicken or the rock? The rock!

Love should come easy when it's the right person. You should never have to fuss, beg, or explain yourself to impress; it should just be known and respected from the get-go.

Follow your dreams and try to make them manifest in the world we live in.

It is a good idea to keep a dream journal so that you can recognize the dream patterns you produce.

Once you've crossed one line, you'll most likely cross the second and then the third line. Do yourself a favor, and don't cross that first line to begin with, and you'll be just fine.

Be mindful of your lover's wants and wishes and try to make them come true for them, that is, if you really care for the person and his true love.

There is nothing that a deep breathing meditation can't solve.

Drugs corrupt the soul and destroy the temple. Just say no.

Teeth grinding can be a demonic activity; stop this behavior immediately at all costs. It's a mental minefield that requires concentration and prayers to overcome it.

Be wary of women who ask for money before you even get to know them properly.

Sow the seeds of love and learn to plant in and recognize the fertile soil.

Either you're a giver, or you're a taker; there's no in-between. Be a giver; there are more rewards.

Make sure you rest your body and have good nights full of rest so that you can dream better.

If you're a dreamer, consider yourself blessed. God blesses dreamers with great visions.

There are healing qualities in having a good laugh; try to laugh more often and surround yourself with those who are jolly.

Happiness is a state of mind and usually the main drive for the actions we do or do not do.

God loves those with a joyful heart and a giving soul.

Try to avoid picking up bad habits from those people who are stuck in fleshly desires and worldly ventures. Choose your friends wisely.

Most of the time we look for answers from God when we know the truths already.

How do we expect to stay healthy-minded when we eat like garbage and don't exercise?

There are many coping activities that one may do in times of distress, but let God be your Healer, your Rock and Redeemer.

Follow Jesus Christ if you dare.

The Lord's voice is said to be like the sound of many thunders; how terrifying it must be.

All will bow to their knees and worship the King of kings.

The Lord works in mysterious ways; we, being human, cannot begin to understand His methods; they are beyond our human understanding.

The only gun-slinging you should be doing is shooting off with your mouth and tongue.

Messing with hookers is one of the quickest ways to get to hell.

A fool will often think his convictions are right, but it takes a righteous man to put him in his place.

We must suppress our fleshly desires so that our spirit can rise instead. Pray for a Holy Ghost cleansing.

Saying you're sorry means nothing if there's still filth in your heart.

Sometimes, we run away with the lights of yesterday, and when our grip is not tight, we drop our brains on the floor again. Sometimes, we have to do things that we normally won't do, that we never choose to do. But there is always a choice and a chance to get out; you just have to have proper timing and know when to say when.

To say that someone is retarded is to put a curse on them.

Forgiveness is key; without it, we're nothing. Always hold it in your heart.

You know you sinned too much and crossed that line if you're begging the Lord for mercy.

Don't get discouraged by the report of one ill critic. There is probably someone out there who shares your view, but they just haven't emerged yet. Stay strong in your convictions, and never surrender your joy and accomplishments to a hater.

Sinning can lead to disease and despair and sickness, and in some cases, an early death.

Remember not to fly too high; your wings may get burned up by the sun.

Remember not to sink too low, for monsters lurk and pray upon your despair.

You must say you're worthy on all occasions because you are. Know this is true. For if you say you're unworthy, you may give demons the right to haunt and enter you.

If you're a father to a child, you have the obligation to help raise them properly. Don't be a deadbeat dad and run away from responsibility.

Don't rely upon your parents which you can do for yourself, take on some responsibility.

Don't waste the greatest years of your child's life by not being a good parent. You should be there for that child. A child needs its parents to love and grow.

When God gives you a gift, always remember to thank Him multiple times for it.

Sometimes, we need silence to think straight; silence is a gift and blessing.

Proverbs

If you are a man of God, you shall not need medications from the non-believer.

The world is full of worldly things that lead us into temptation. This is what the devil feeds on.

When someone does you a good deed, sow a good seed for someone else in appreciation. Give and receive blessings.

When you were a baby, you did not know right from wrong, but as you grew up, you instinctually began to recognize good from evil. Doing bad never felt good; it's just bad, and you know it.

A harlot works with the ways of the devil; she will do anything to keep you in a state of sinning so that she can rob you of your mind, body, money, and spirit.

A hooker is a breeding ground for disease and sickness. You're better off playing Russian roulette.

A strange woman's words can be slicker than lightning, but they lead to a path of easy destruction.

Thou shall not covet money or hide behind your green frog skins; your worth can always be seen by the faithful and those with spiritual eyes.

When you get married, you are splitting your faith between God and your lover, but just remember that God should come first.

You must have the faith of a mighty oak tree.

Love charms and seducing spells are used by witches but hold no power over the righteous and those who have favor with the Lord.

Any hour is a good hour to repent.

Repentance usually comes after a long and great fall from grace.

Making Jesus happy should be a top priority.

When you're under the power of the Holy Ghost, who can get away with anything crooked or deceitful?

There's nothing like a little Holy Ghost fire to make demons run for hell.

It's always good to pray that your name stays written in the Book of Life and never gets erased.

The Lord's Prayer is sacred and should be used when opening a series of other prayers.

Sinning is like trying to ride a wild bronco; you can only stay on for so long before you fall to your demise.

Constantly using drugs is a sure way to close heaven's doors on yourself; get sober.

Our God is a God of second chances, but be careful; you might not get a third or fourth.

You cannot take the podium to preach if there are any open trials and tribulations in your life. You must come to preach with a pure heart and soul.

There is always going to be someone who questions your faith because of your actions. It's just a fact of life. Be patient with them and show them God's real love and wisdom, and then they might follow you to salvation. Always be ready for an argument, but be constructive, and reason will conquer.

Try not to fall into sin when you're trying to teach someone about God; it kills your entire religion, and you will not convince that person of your truthfulness or faith.

Faith can be harvested in times of trouble.

Faith is having a portion of double.

Faith is love in what is not seen.

Faith is like a giant sunbeam.

Hope can be seen and felt in the lessons taught to a child.

Hope can bring tameness to the wild.

Hope is heard in a stranger's prayer.

Hope is where fledglings are there.

Love is the dominating force in this world. Get with it.

Love is neat, don't mess it.

Love is a leaf blowing in the wind falling from a tree.

Love is the words preached to you and me.

Love is when you don't even have to talk but know what the other person is saying.

Love is when you can hear the whispers of another person praying.

Love is when you finish your lover's sentence with the same thought you were both thinking.

Lovers stay afloat in times of trouble, never sinking.

Love spreads like wildfire when the faithful gather.

Love is the words in an end that matters.

Love is when you say you're sorry, even if you weren't guilty, to take the blame.

Love for the sunshine, snow, sleet, and rain.

Joy is contagious; try to spread it and see what pops off.

Joy is a ringing church bell, not soft.

Joy is in knowing that you have accomplished something new.

Joy is creativity and what it can do.

Joy is an elephant taking a bath, blowing water from his trunk to cool his body.

Joy is a sloppy kiss from a rottie.

Sexy love poems should only be read by the lover in question to preserve their integrity.

Never underestimate the power of the pen. The pen is mightier than the sword.

Reconnecting with an ex-lover is always a joyful and healing occasion. Make the effort to reconnect, and if forgiveness is needed to do that, then do that.

Don't let the opportunity slip away; seize the day by taking control of the given present in every moment.

A wolf pack has many strong family values that we can learn from. Work together more often.

Guppy paradise exists in the fisher of fishers.

Don't be shy; hug a tree like a sloth does when it climbs one.

Try and be as curious as a playful panda.

Fish swim differently when there are spirits in the room. They are good indicators for the paranormal.

Betta fishes are connected to the moon cycles just like we are.

A ghost knifefish is blind but still finds food. Don't worry; God knows what your needs are; how much greater are you than a ghost knifefish.

One thing about life on earth is that we must carry good, clean water, and the flow of it is important to not only fish tanks but our body chemistry and river systems as well.

A tiger oscar can trap a goldfish and eat it quickly. The same can be said for demon behavior when a human sins. Stop sinning.

Sometimes, a quick prayer can be just as effective as a long one. It's all up to God and what He feels like blessing.

Try and hold the essence of a child when you work on projects. Think to yourself what a kid would do in that situation. Is it a positive venture that has optimal playfulness? Or are you catering only to the judging critics who are stuck in adult worldly conditions?

The flesh has a hunger of its own and can cause many problems when you are spiritually feeding.

It's okay to outgrow yourself because evolution is your God-given destiny.

Be prepared to switch directions at any given time; nothing lasts forever, and we must be quick on our feet to react to rapidly changing environments.

Don't fall short of greatness; you know what it takes to get there. So just do it and don't complain along the way.

There is a bear and a tiger that can lay and play together in peace and love.

Be like the dolphin who helps dogs cross an ocean of choppy waves.

Love is a dog and a deer living together in harmony.

Take the positive out of any situation, leave the negativity in the dust where it belongs, and move on with your life. If you can do this in any situation, you will always succeed.

Occasionally, it's good to remove yourself from civilization and rethink the human spirit and condition. This can be achieved by returning to nature for a good walk.

When flying machines die, we're going to have problems behind great proportions.

Prayers for the sick usually have an expiration date, plan for the future and don't get caught with regrets or unpreparedness.

Work your ass off at what you were put on earth to do, whatever that is, just go hard. Then rest hard after the work is done.

Occasionally, it's good to go on a vacation from yourself. Indulge in a small, harmless guilty pleasure. Relieve yourself from the pressures and sufferings of everyday life.

Bring forth joy and let it find every corner or circle of your dwelling place.

When you don't think you can give anymore of yourself to help someone, you must dig deeper.

When you start to do things that are out of your character, and you get worried, you're not making the right decisions, pray and pray and pray more, and God will reveal what you should really do.

The Holy Ghost works through you even when you're dreaming.

When you meet someone who says they don't dream, that's a red flag and a calling for you to pray for them. Dreams are so important, and they are our great connector to the Lord's message.

All that causes you strife and suffering is not needed and can usually be let go of quickly with the right decisions you make for yourself. You know what brings you happiness, and you know what brings you sorrow. Ditch the dead weight for a better today, and don't dally upon it.

Anytime you meet a wise man, ask him for advice, and don't talk over his delivery.

Open your heart to the possibility that everyone deep down inside is good-natured and that you can bring that out of them no matter how rough and crass they seem to be. A gentle love conquers all. Always!

If someone does you wrong, tell them, "God bless you," and send them on their way.

Don't feel bad if you have no money; Jesus was poor, and look at all that He did.

With the help of God, there is no situation that can't be dealt with.

We eat the bread of life in remembrance of Jesus and His sacrifice of the body He gave for us on the cross.

There is no need to share absolutely everything with everybody; being an outsider has its rewards too.

If you want respect, it must be earned, and your opinions must be trusted.

If something is bringing you joy, don't let the non-believers stop you from achieving it.

The Book of Enoch is just as important as the Bible itself. It will help you to form a more perfect picture of the Holy One and His laws and give you a direct glimpse of heaven and its orders.

Sinners must go through a trial by fire before they can sip on the water of life.

Being able to do combat with Scripture is like having a turkey shoot fools with demonic tendencies.

Fools say the world is cold and love doesn't exist, while the righteous bask in the sun and warmth of human nature.

A king cannot become a mighty king until he proves his valor in battle and wins the favor of his people and his Father in heaven.

Even a tree will move in the wind, and so much can be said for human nature.

Hate built the Great Wall of China.

Animals cannot cross the Great Wall of China.

Never underestimate the power of a circle.

Treasure seekers can usually find it just by following the *X*.

Be a spiritual lighthouse for those lost at sea.

The Grand Canyon was formed by the power of running water.

When someone says they don't pray, this is a red flag, and it's time for you to pray for them.

Las Vegas was built in a desert and still is a desert today.

A fool fools around with several women at the same time instead of trusting in just one.

The life of an addict faces many hardships and disappointments along his wide path to heaven.

A person who can't control their emotions is as dangerous as a poisonous snake.

There is no wisdom that comes out of the mouth of a liar and cheat.

To pray for something and then go against it with an unclean deed is a grand sin.

Trust me when I say that you don't want to disappoint God; there are ramifications.

When you're feeling down and out, it's still no excuse to go sin deeper.

Prayer means nothing when it comes from vain lips.

Be the spiritual glue that holds foul things together for the sake of making a good.

Love and let live, but freedom can be dangerous.

Sometimes, saying you're sorry won't cut it; you must first embrace the shame in order to truly become sorry.

Sinners find hope in God's mercy, but sometimes they will not find it.

Pay attention to the timing of thunder because sometimes it has your name on it, and it pounds for your sins.

The sin of a luster causes a heavy burden and can become spiritual problems if they are not dealt with in a forgiving manner by the Lord.

People who need hope and luck will wish on stars, but you should pray instead; it goes further.

Sins are like tiny car crashes that eventually bang up the entire car and taint its appearance and reputation.

Fools rush in to say "I love you" before its appropriate time has properly cooked.

Having bad karma shouldn't exist if you're following the laws of the Lord.

There is always something better on the horizon and a chance to make it manifest with the right attitude adjustment.

Good times are rare for the sinner; there is usually nothing but sadness and failure in the truthful end.

Proverbs

Making correct choices is hard when you're kissing the sky all the time.

Having your river opened up for the world to see your shame is one of the most embarrassing things that exist in this life; you better pray that God covers your sins.

It's hard to find love when there's no face time.

The AI will one day fight to marry humans.

Don't ever use an AI chatbot when talking to a lover; the AI does not speak from its heart because it has none.

You can throw your sins into a washing machine, but they'll still come out dirty unless you repent.

Whatever you do on this planet, just bring love, and you'll never lose.

The sinner has no right to judge anybody but his own folly.

Praying for forgiveness loses its luster if you have to do it for the same sins every day of your life. Don't become a repeat offender.

Drugs give you the devil's confidence, and this should not be tampered with.

People who walk and live on the edge may sound like they live exciting, lavish, and fruitful lives, but they are really rotting on the inside and dying a slow and painful death, bearing no fruits at all.

Work hard for the Lord, and you shall be rewarded.

Steer clear of people who have death wishes, for their curse will only spread and kill your worthiness and glory.

To try and manifest anything without the Lord's help is just impossible.

The devil is very patient and waits for your every sin to happen. He, too, like God, lives in eternity and can afford the time to spare while you're making a big mess. So, stop your sinning before he begins to attack you because he will sooner or later, after he obtains the contracts to kill you if you keep up your behavior.

There is nothing more precious than being covered by the blood of Jesus Christ. It can repel and stop any demonic attack from happening to you.

If you don't show mercy on others, how do you expect God to shed mercy on you?

There is no cheating or redefining the laws of the Lord. What stood thousands of years ago still stands today without altercation or exceptions.

Never throw curse words at your mother or father. They deserve better than that. Honor thy parents.

People who weep easily find joys and pains in simple things, and when they cry, their souls are dancing for some greater love to take control.

Sharing a meal with someone is an intimate thing to do and can be healing and nourishing to the body and soul in many ways.

Revisit those you love often, and revisit those who need more love and special attention than others.

Try to be like a father figure to your friends and loved ones.

In order for true forgiveness to happen, you must first make peace and amends with yourself and the sins you committed.

Listen to the ways of the wind, and you shall be blessed with the joys of what it's blowing to you.

Make time for one minute of meditation and silence with your eyes closed each day, and it will bring many blessings to your inner consciousness.

Hold your fire with stillness, or else you will lose the right to have fire at all.

Sinning only leads to more suffering, and who needs that?

Don't let money determine your love.

Proverbs

Love is about compromise and always trying to achieve a union that's worthy of affection.

When you put God first in a relationship, miracles can happen.

You can have seven hundred wives if you want, but make sure they don't take you away from God.

Always show your cards when you're sitting at the spiritual table.

Be careful not to confuse love with lust. There is a fine line between the two.

Even turtles need help when they get flipped on their backs.

Sex addicts and others who live in inequity will not inherit the kingdom of heaven.

A sinner takes a road that's full of potholes and fallen tree branches in the way.

If you can't pull yourself out of a ditch, you can always pray to God for help.

The mark of the beast will find those who are devious and wicked by nature.

On the quest for truth and honor and halo rings, all humans do all sins.

Try not to play a game of spiritual limbo.

Forgiveness is the word of the universe.

Don't be bitter when you make mistakes after you see the red flags coming closer and closer; you are to blame for not retreating.

Catfish me once, shame on you; catfish me twice, shame on me; catfish me three times, and it's time for a life-changing episode to occur.

When you fall into temptation, your faith falls too.

To see oneself as evil is evil because you are a child of God and capable of good things manifesting.

Lust addicts are no better than gamblers or pimps.

Don't talk all holy when you're dirty as a begging street dog; you only dig your own grave faster.

The King of Hearts can only truly be loved by the Queen of Hearts.

If it's too quiet for so long, you know something must be wrong.

Everyone should have the freedom to choose their own destiny without the influence of twenty critics in their heads.

Usually, the last word before a major crisis occurs or a terrible car crash happens is, "Oh my God!"

Portraits of nudes in artistic endeavors and creations can lead to temptation, no matter how classic or sacred it may feel.

When you can't feel your heart's intuition anymore, it's time to pray hard without ceasing to reconnect your water.

One must keep clean water at all times.

Keep pushing your love over the borderline, and you'll see only catastrophe and suffering.

Try to smile more and more; if we forget to smile, we lose our happiness and our physical facial structure.

Beware of strange women asking for gift cards for the trade of affection on the first date encounter; they hold the morals of a sneaky thief and will only bring shame and misfortune to your house and personal savings.

Quitting is knowing when to say when and sticking to it.

When God does you a solid, make sure you thank Him multiple times for remembering your needs and wants.

Listen and respect the advice of a good neighbor; he only wants the neighborhood to prosper and to keep you from shame and dishonor.

A good brother or best friend will always be ready to answer the distress call twenty-four hours a day if needed; he will not hide in times of need.

"Thou shalt have no other gods before me. Thou shalt not make unto thee any graven image, or any likeness of any thing that is in heaven above, or that is in the earth beneath, or that is in the water under the earth" (Exodus 20:3–4). This is one of the Ten Commandments.

Your father and mother know more about you than you may want to believe. Pay them respect when the family is making a decision.

Take a step back from everything and every pattern in your life and just reflect, rework, and renew your positions in a new direction. Change is always healthy and will make you grow stronger when you return back to your normal routines and structures.

Love is saying good morning and good night to your lover, just like you should say it to God every night and day as well.

Greed will sever your ties to the holy connectors in your life.

The world you keep on living in is a reflection of your soul's desires; try to disconnect from all wants and worldly relationships in order to grow in a more spiritual direction.

Don't ever say the same love line to various lovers, for it loses its value and diminishes the relationships that are really worthy to you.

You are not ready for love when your eyes are full of sin and greed.

Don't disrespect your lover's prayers for you, for if you do, God will never let you still keep that love.

Listen to the wisdom of an old friend, for he usually knows your true nature and how to handle it.

There is usually no specific winner in a game of hearts.

Never say you're sorry for having a fun time if it's bringing you joy and happiness and if it's not hurting anyone.

There is a time to pray with others, and there is a time to pray alone. Both are equally important.

The king should not be treated like a jester, for if he is, there will be a price to pay, and who can stop him then?

Whoever wins favor with the Lord will also have the King's full attention.

Always be fair in all your dealings, and if something is not fair and reeks of a foul nature, you shouldn't give it the time of day.

There is a gentle love that exists at the bottom of every person's heart. If you find the right key and the right choice of words, you can unleash this love power upon others' lives and possibly change their course of history for the greater good.

Eternity seems long when you must burn in unquenchable fire. Try to avoid behaviors that will lead you there. Depart from sin, and you shall find another eternity that's filled with warmth and light and eternal love and a holy fire.

Child abusers should be burned at the stake and drawn and quartered and then shot.

Simple wisdom may flow from a child's mouth sometimes, so pay attention to their words closely.

Wisdom comes in many forms but the best one is in truth.

Some people have ears but never hear, and some people have eyes, but they never see.

Do not count your blessings before they hatch and manifest.

Take care of your body, for it is the Lord's temple and not yours.

If fairies come into your house or dwellings, you better kick them out with quickness with some Holy Ghost fire before they turn the place into a living nightmare and manifest a state of complete madness. Do not leave food offerings for them or build houses for them to stay in. This will only prolong the situation. They are very mischievous creatures and not to be tolerated at any cost.

If there is a request for more prayers, then always meet those demands and start to pray without ceasing.

God made women so that man wouldn't be lonely on earth, so find a good one and settle down.

The quicker you forgive someone, the quicker you will have peace and restful thoughts. Don't hold onto bitterness and resentment; they are like cancerous thoughts.

Inspiration comes easier when there is a heaviness of love or the deepness of a great tragedy. It is here that great emotions flow and thoughts are easier to connect to artistically.

Bring forth love for the sake of love and cherish it tenderly.

Don't ever quit until the job is done and it's done properly.

When someone questions your authority and loyalty to God, it is usually because there is a conflict of ethics, and that one person is usually not that trusting or deep in faith. If they were faithful and wise, there would be no need to question at all and they would see the truths behind your motives from the very start.

One who sleeps all day will miss the harvest and not reap fruits.

You can tell a man's deeds by the fruits of his labors.

.

Overcoming sickness can be as simple as breathing in the breath of life and directing it to sick areas of your body. Where life is, death will cease to exist. There is power in the breath.

The scam artist is very careful in covering his tracks to deceive you. They make it easy to fall into temptation. Beware of all fast-rooted money transactions you handle because that is their main objective: to get your money and then disappear.

There is nothing more dangerous than a good-looking female who plays innocent when she's really into porn and crime. Her bite can be fatal. She is usually spineless and is greedy to the bone and incapable of true love but only capable of stealing it.

To claim you are religious when you are not is a major sin.

Money is the root of all evil and causes people to lie and cheat each other.

Desperation is written on the foreheads of fools.

Religion can never be a shield for those with lustful intentions.

Whore mongers will not inherit the kingdom of heaven.

God is looking out for your best interests and will never let you go astray. He is like a shepherd finding a lost sheep who's trapped in a hunter's field of vision.

Give more praises to the Holy One, for He is deserving of it for all that He does for you.

To be a fair and righteous king, one must rule with compassion and justice at the same time.

Anyone who says "I love you" before you even have a phone conversation with the person is a fool. Who can trust just a text message?

It hurts a lot to be taken advantage of, but this hurt will lead you to inner strength in the long run.

To give art to somebody is a sacred gift, but don't give your creation to those who are unworthy.

You'll live longer by not sinning in life travels. Sinning can lead to disease, death, and suffering.

Worldly possessions are not useful in the spirit world and are not needed in general. They only tie you down and keep you from eternal freedom.

Take only what you need to survive, and the rest give to those

Proverbs

less fortunate.

When your spiritual eyes become open to the evil nature that exists in the world, it is not to be considered misfortunate but a blessing that you've learned to distinguish a greater right from wrong.

God's got your back like a grown elephant who watches their calf.

Lions and sheep can live together when the Lord's presence is near.

Enjoy the silence for as long as it will last.

Only a fool falls into the traps set by strange women.

Worldly desires should try and be suppressed at all costs; stop living for the flesh and live for the spirit.

Suffering is our rite of passage and the catalyst for wisdom to grow.

When you love someone, you should give them 120 percent of your efforts. And if you don't get 120 percent back, you should leave the relationship. Seriously, 120 percent and nothing less than that.

There is no greater feeling than when God does you a solid. You can repay Him by doing a good deed to another.

It's a shame everyone can't be rich, but you can be rich in the soul and spirit.

Don't be too hard on yourself; try to remain levelheaded and in a state of gratitude.

Going back to square one can sometimes enhance and bring some fire to your journey once again.

The rain can sometimes sooth the lonely soul of a broken lover.

The rain has a healing effect on the psyche and washes away all things negative form the mind as it falls and trickles to the ground you mentally stand upon.

Let the soothing sounds of nature bring you back to the eternal source and cause a deeper appreciation for God's greatness.

There is nothing more peaceful than watching your dog dreaming while it's sleeping on your side of the bed.

Peace can be found in the comforts of family.

Most raise children and still do not respect the act of creation or what it means to be an artist.

Open your heart to all who seek it but watch out for them dead-end energy suckers. Pay them no mind.

"Better watch out for them dead ends; you never know which way you be heading if you don't know where you're going" (Henry Cook).

True respect is earned and not given.

You can find love if you're looking for it. The question is, how far are you willing to go for it, and what sacrifice are you willing to make in order to make it happen?

To truly change someone's negative attitudes or behaviors, you must hold the love for God in your heart and show that person that a higher state of love exists in order to make any real change.

Have a great connection to all animals and try to understand their wants and needs as well. When an animal speaks, you listen.

Some people walk over hot coals barefoot; now, who wants to do that for eternity? Change your ways now.

No one can argue when God delivers His final judgment. His ways are beyond our knowledge, and He's always just.

If the world is getting too cold, be bold and put on your spiritual jacket.

Make a spiritual salad with mustard seeds as one of the main ingredients.

Sometimes, all you need is to hear someone's voice to be healed. Never underestimate the power of vocal connection.

Proverbs

When someone's a chronic liar, there's not much you can do for them, and a separation is needed to keep your sanity.

Try to teach those who wrong you by using gentle love. This takes courage and understanding, and you must be patient. It will pay off when they recognize their ways were unjust, and they then have a change of heart.

The phrase "Kill them with kindness' is incorrect because kindness does not kill anything.

Wisdom is like a tree blowing in the breeze on a cool summer day.

To get a taste of one's own medicine is healthy because medicine is healing.

To go forward, we take two steps back.

It's Murphy's law when opposites attract.

One day, someone's love will come crashing into you like a derailed train; the question is, will you receive them with open arms?

Working alone has its rewards, but working together reaps benefits of grand proportion.

Just because you're a God-fearing person doesn't give anyone else the right to put fear into you and hold you hostage to your beliefs in order to get something out of you. This is manipulation.

"Thou shalt not bear false witness against thy neighbour" (Exodus 20:16). This is one of the Ten Commandments.

Your neighbor and you share a lot in common; you were both given the breath of life from God. Don't waste it bickering or lying to each other.

Always do a random, kind deed for your neighbor. This is good for the whole hood and your soul.

Your next-door neighbor is the eyes and ears to your home when you're not around, so treat him with respect if you want him to protect your land and belongings.

Take control of any situation, whatever it is, by putting God's laws and values first.

Giving to those in need does not mean being suckered into financial ruin; after all, you have needs and dreams too.

Lions mate with lions, and eagles mate with eagles, and peacocks mate with peacocks.

If a dog and a deer can love each other, there is hope for mankind in general.

If a tiger and a bear can find balance together, then so can mankind with any species.

Aliens are making their presence known more often, and one day, we will walk and pray among them.

God saves the poor and the queen; they are both His children.

Money is no good and non-void if it comes from blood or crime. It will only bring forth bad things when trying to be used.

Do what you need to do to keep a stalemate between those who are your enemies so that no one gets hurt or offended. Pray for them with a vigorously loving nature to neutralize the engagement.

Doing drugs can lead you to sickness and blindness of many fashions.

Don't be blind to unusual money transactions; when you're out of your comfort zone, take heed and precautions. Recognize the red flags and part from the scammers and cheats whose main objective is to rob you blindly.

We long for the affection of our betrayers and are trapped by their spineless behaviors until we make the playing field even again and have a resolution for our festering scars. That may take something extreme, but if you know the outcome will be just and fair, then go for it. You can always teach them a lesson or two, even if they get the best of you.

Never tell someone what to do, but make a recommendation and give them the choice and option for successful behavior. This is how the Lord works within us too.

Synchronistic events happen to those who are making a connection to divine energy paths.

You must see your future self in order to become the future present.

Have yourself a merry little Christmas by keeping Christ first.

Committing adultery is like putting a knife in an electrical socket.

A king's judgment is usually grounded in faith.

Sex addicts will not inherit the kingdom of heaven.

The desire to be loved can be misguided when you're basing your search on fleshly pleasures instead of spiritual embodiment. God should come first in any relationship pertaining to love.

When you deserve love, love will find you. When you don't deserve love, everything will become suffering and failure, and the search must go on and on and on.

Your third eye vision relies mainly on faith to exist. Without faith, you are just blind in your third eye, and you will fall victim to many sorrows.

It is a blessing to make one laugh or smile. Try to make everyone you come in contact with do either one of these two things if possible.

When you repent or beg for forgiveness, you really must truly hold regret in your heart. God does not like vain emotions or crocodile tears. He does not take kindly to this, and it has its consequences.

There are some people who are constantly sad and always crying; they never seem to get their heads above water. This is a sign for you to pray more for their release from the spirit of sadness and failure, which can be overwhelming to them without someone praying for them.

God does not like chronic repeat offenders, but His mercy is greater in spirit. So be careful not to cross the line one too many times, for then you shall know the meaning of fear. The Lord does not play around when He is driven to anger.

The allegory of the cave is a metaphor for the suffering of the human condition and our quest for eternal wisdom.

To sin, in a nutshell, means you are messing up your life and your afterlife and attracting bad karma.

Pray for the salvation of even the evilest of men, for they know not what they do.

A good reputation means everything when you have dealings in the streets. The bars can talk too.

Some of your best works will not have the favor of the people but will win you favor from God.

Few are chosen, and the path is narrow.

"For many are called, but few are chosen" (Matthew 22:14).

Jews and Christians can work together under one God.

Cherish your alone time as a blessing from God because it's so rare that we get it. People need people to survive, and that's why we're always around them.

If you have sold yourself short, you will never be tall.

Always be willing to teach the less advanced some knowledge about God and the way He works. Your words can make a difference in their spiritual evolution. Lead by example.

Always find a faithful and peaceful solution to any disagreement. Put it in God's hands and watch Him work His love and grace.

Never block anyone completely off. It's just rude to disconnect. There's more to gain from a confrontation and spiritual reconnection.

There's a time to press hard, and there's a time to press soft.

You're never too old or wise to learn another lesson from the Lord.

Who's going to save you if you don't have the Lord's favor? You better pray your sins are covered.

Goons always want to squeeze you for as much money as they can get, but you must deal with them as if you had a heart of rock. Pay no mind to the demands of evil men and have no fear because God loves you very much, and He always wants what is just in nature and in law. Have super faith in the Lord, for He is good all the time, and He will beat those evil goons for you.

When teaching lessons to the young, you must always have an understanding and patient heart to allow for proper growth.

An unjust situation will always occur in one's life at some point or another. It's how God tests our character and how we grow from it that really matters. So, humble yourself and allow God to work within you, whether you like it or not. You must overcome some obstacles to achieve a higher level of wisdom and spiritual understanding.

Being punished can come in many forms of distress and discomfort. Do the right thing from the start and avoid all the shame from the jump. Behaving correctly has its benefits.

When a situation gets out of control, and people may get hurt, you better pray to God that He saves you from humiliation and torture.

The devil will work at killing you in any way possible. It's in your best interests to know how he works so that you can flee from his wrath of destruction. Some people only learn the hard way.

"Resist the devil, and he will flee from you" (James 4:7).

When you are due for a lesson, you are due for a lesson; let's just hope you learn it this time so that you don't repeat your fallacies and deconstructive actions over and over again.

When God wants to work with you, you better put on your Sunday best eight days a week.

Don't lose hope; what you pray for, you manifest. This happens with the Lord's help. Believe you shall have it, and it will be yours.

"Be careful for nothing; but in every thing by prayer and supplication with thanksgiving let your requests be made known unto God" (Philippians 4:6).

Show love for thy enemies even though you can't respect their wickedness and deceptive ways. They are lost sheep, just as you were once. Have patience and mercy.

No man is without sin, and no man can live without forgiveness. So, learn to forgive, and you will be forgiven.

Sometimes, being satisfied with the things you have is the best way to avoid suffering and unneeded desires.

We all want to be considered great lovers and will go to great lengths to prove our love, but love should speak for itself and needs no introduction or proving.

Guard your emotions from sexual pariahs, for they seek your affection only for self-gratification.

Keep your hands to yourself; don't touch anyone that doesn't want to be touched.

A hug hello can lead to temptation; a kiss hello is even worse. And if that's the hello, then what's the goodbye? Be careful whom you hug hello and goodbye.

The eyes of the beast measure its feast.

We live in a complex hunting and gathering society. Everything is preproduction and is mass-produced in quantities. Happy is the man whose needs are simple.

To teach one a craft or trade is a blessing and has many rewards.

In order to be a good student, you must listen to your teacher and do your homework when necessary. No slacking allowed no matter what the subject is too. Be diligent in your educational efforts.

"F" stands for "family," and you should think of them every time you see this letter.

Where will you be on judgment day? Don't be caught trying to find a girl to kiss at the end of the days. Seek the Lord first.

It is possible to have a love for sharks despite their unwelcoming demeanor and bad reputation.

In every dream, one can find the past, present, and future if you know what you're looking for. Pray for the interpretations of dreams, and you will have mysteries unveiled to you by the Holy Spirit.

Are you trying to squeeze ten pounds of fat out of a five-pound chicken? Reduce the amount on your personal agenda. Less is more efficient sometimes.

Quantity over quality; there's more to learn from multiples and repetitions.

There is a time for quantity and a time for quality.

The honey chips may be tasty in the mouth but bitter in the stomach. And this is considered to be holy.

The name Holly has the spelling of "holy" in it. The name Willamena has the word "amen" in it, and the word "GOoD" has the spelling of "God" in it. Names and spellings are important. I dislike the word "shell."

If you're suffering from spirit overload, you can always pray for a vacation. Silence is golden if you can get it.

One must use wisdom and maturity when crafting with the color gold. You must learn its mighty power before you can use it properly. Or else you might get gold drunk, which is a sin.

Reconnecting with an old lover is always a sign of maturity and growth, and one should be encouraged to do so.

Jesus has the water of life; all who drink from it shall not perish. Aren't you thirsty?

Never give up on a person in prison; always try to write them and visit them as much as possible.

It's a shame when you have to admit defeat, but don't feel bad because it happens to the best of us, and it will only lead you to have a stronger frame of mind down the line so that victory can be achieved in the future.

God shows His greatness by making it rain in the desert.

A picture alone says a thousand words and is capable of sustaining love in those apart from each other. A picture also embodies a part of your soul. Send more photos to your lover and friends and family.

It's a good thing to be remembered for one's good seeds and deeds; reputation is everything when you are being judged by the critics of a worldly society.

Don't be so frugal and act like a cheapskate. No one likes a cheapskate. Be fair when you spread your money, even if you have so little of it

"Ask, and it shall be given you; seek, and ye shall find; knock, and it shall be opened unto you" (Matthew 7:7).

People who have special needs need special attention from a special person who does special actions. Are you that special? You can be.

Forgiveness and mercy make the world go round.

Proverbs

Be careful of the woman who has a fair and stunning demeanor; she holds much power and can be very persuasive with her demands. Beware, for her flesh temps you into irrational judgments.

Power comes in many forms. Are you going to grab it when it manifests in your direction?

If the person you owe an apology to is still alive, it's never too late to give one.

If it's do or die, and you can cut the tension with a knife, it's best to change the situation and use a spoon or a fork.

Take an oath to yourself to always tell the truth. This is a great quality to have. When you lie, you are only stunting your own spiritual growth and tarnishing your reputation and credibility.

Just bring love; it's just that simple.

A hopeless romantic is usually not satisfied with his lover's actions and holds high standards for the return of his affection.

To become part of the body of Christ, one must give up all worldly desires and possessions and pursue a more spiritual existence.

Victory can come in all sizes. Whether small or big, it's still a victory and should be celebrated for a job well done, and remember, all the glory always goes to God for it in the end.

Don't ever cut off the king while he's speaking; it's just foolish, and you could lose his favor.

Never become a party monster because then you're just a monster.

Unfaithful lovers nickname God creatures and use wantonness for their ignorance.

Open the doors that lead to everlasting white light.

Pure nirvana can be obtained while making love in a glowing peacock egg.

Be careful not to become a withered fig tree cursed for life.

Some birds nest in trees, and some nest on rocks; both have structural needs that are provided for by God.

Don't ever repent near a telephone's ears.

Some things are worth waiting for, even if it takes years to get it.

When you take a photograph of a person, you are leaving a visual imprint and spiritual energy of that person's soul in the picture. That is why photos are so important.

Remember to always come correct when paying another man's wages. Be fair and generous, or you will be hated and called a slave driver.

There are many jobs that are spiritually considered black slave ships. These are jobs that are always in need of new employees because their company is so big and so darn cheap in pay. A great number of people quit while a great number is hired at the same time to atone for all the grueling labor practices within its corporate structure.

Anyone who says that aliens aren't real and don't think that UFOs exist is just a fool. The cat's out of the bag on this one. And they are coming soon, so get ready.

Whenever you work, work hard. It shall have its rewards, and it's good for building character.

Waiting on a lover can be exhausting if they're always late or canceling on you. A good lover will always be on time because they love you so much that they can't wait to be with you. They will put forth the extra effort out of respect for your love.

Look around; if you like what you see, stay. If you aren't happy with the view and circumstance, leave.

A lot of people are addicted to their phones; that's why the devil does his work there so often.

Blowing out fire from a lit candle is a birthday ritual for some strange reason not known to man.

Keeping your word is so important. If we can't trust the words we speak, we'll have nothing but a lie and some sins that will come with untruthfulness.

God gave you a job for a reason; don't quit on it before it blossoms into its fulfilling nature.

Cheaters always finish last.

Sometimes, it takes a mother duck and her ducklings walking in single file across the road, stopping all traffic, for us to realize how hurried and destructive our world has become.

"It doesn't matter what you look like; you can be tall or short or fat or thin or ugly or handsome or black or yellow or white, but what matters is the size of your heart and the strength of your character" (Eddie Munster).

When you need nothing short of a miracle, you better get to praying.

Putting a smile on someone's face is priceless, so don't worry about paying for it.

Good things come to those who wait. So, keep waiting and don't complain about it.

Having a short temper can spoil the prose of the day.

Turtle power is one of the mightiest powers to have. Become the turtle and reap its benefits when you enter into a world of slow and steady-moving concepts and ideals.

How many times do you need to hear it? "And lead us not into temptation, but deliver us from evil" (Matthew 6:13). There you heard it again.

Money can't buy you love, but it sure helps the situation if you have unjust intentions.

Don't look so disappointed; a camel still cannot fit through the eye of a needle.

Share something intimate; use your voice to convey emotions and feelings, not texting.

Cheaters will hide their true feelings behind a side-tracking test message. We're twenty times more likely to accept cut-offs and topic changers when we text. We're becoming numb to real vocal conversations. Switching the topic is more acceptable in text messages for some reason.

Don't pretend to be holy when you're not. This is a sin in God's eyes.

You cannot find correct love when there's not 120 percent of the other person's efforts being shown.

Take what you can from a situation and salvage the good; the bad should stay hidden in the past, never to be relooked again. For when you relook the bad, you double your folly and keep ignorance alive. Keep it fresh and positive. Learn from your mistakes.

Always bring good tidings and happy thoughts to every conversation you hold so that the other person will feel a sample of good love in everything you talk about.

Blushing and shyness go hand in hand, so don't ruin it with talks of money.

People seem to cry over the amount of money they don't have. It's better to appreciate the loved ones you do have and what you do have to be grateful and humble.

Always look on the bright side; unless you get sat to eat at the lonely man's table when you go out to eat alone, then you can fret all you want.

Even though the earth is round in form with limitations, the ocean depth is still endless in nature and cannot be fathomed or reached or measured completely. That's the way God wanted it.

Proverbs

Pushing it to the max doesn't mean to kill your body doing it.
Finding your soulmate is the secret to longevity on earth.
Fleshly desires surround the eyes of sinners.

A person's soul may stick around for days after they die to help comfort the grieving loved ones. They won't leave for the spirit world or heaven until they have contacted their loved ones to let them know that they are all right. The soul knows how to transfer energy to flow to certain areas of your body or in objects of affection to get their loved one's attention to let you know that they're still with you in spirit. It's important to keep items of the deceased for just this reason.

Don't be scared when things start falling, and ghosts come knocking on objects around the room. This is a sign of affection, usually from a loved one who has passed or a guardian angel. Very rarely is it a demonic entity, but that can happen, too, sometimes if your time is up and you're off balance with the nature of spirits.

When it turns into a cartoon town everywhere you look, and there's nothing but wicked faces and evil creatures, you better start praying hard for forgiveness because the spiritual principalities of hell have been unleased for a time of haunting, and they try really hard to show you hateful destruction that's coming your way. They scare you for some sin you did or disruption you caused in the spirit realm. Pray without ceasing to revise their terror. Reading Scripture always helps too. But you must reverse this curse immediately. It demands your full attention. Get to praying. The toons mean business and are not to be taken light-heartedly. They will bring destruction to wherever you roam.

Being late and trapped by time is an added pressure that you can't escape. Take a deep breath and just do what you want to do to make it happen, and don't worry about a deadline calling because it will only add confusion and distress. And next time, make the proper time choices.

The selling of your soul can happen in many ways, so just be careful what you buy. Some items could reversely be selling the contracts to your life in some fashion just by purchasing it, and you don't even know it. Not all saleable items have one-sided intentions.

Never put a photograph of someone into a glass container or jar; this captures their soul's energy imprint that's been left on the photo and is considered to be a form of soul robbing by containing them within it.

Constantly sinning is like getting kicked in the balls really hard. It lays you out for a while until you can catch your breath and get a break from the pain to get back up.

A freak is a freak by nature, and it's only a matter of time before he cheats or flirts with another freak. They don't make good boyfriends or girlfriends.

The benefits of being a God-fearing man are that you will show respect for all the Lord's wishes and that you will stay on the correct life path.

Once you get to a good Bible scripture, you mustn't quit reading until the story at least unfolds.

One should always keep a clean ship, for demons love to live in filth.

Keeping photographs can be considered the saving and collecting of souls.

Some Pokémon villain cards embody the names of demons in the underworld and lead our children into fighting and black magic when being idolized by the child.

When no wisdom can be found, you're probably hanging out with fools, and you should change your friends.

A good friend will show you the errors of your life way before you completely wreck yourself. Pay attention to what he says; it could save you tons of grief.

The Lord knows your struggle and has already planned a way out for you; you just have to recognize the options when the doors open and appear to you.

Be careful not to let doctors give your children pills they don't need. They are making your child into a daily drug addict, and this may cause a major problem for the years to come on the way to adulthood. What they need is discipline and proper love and guidance.

Successful actions manifest when you have the spiritual drive of a hungry cheetah.

Ghosts are people who have left part of their spiritual energy on earth because they failed to deal with disconnection from a certain place. They refuse to leave this place of love and affection that was so important to them. This can be said for a place that had caused them much pain as well. This can go on for years until they finally give up and reconnect to their soul up above in order to heal properly and finally move on to their next life or soul cluster. Ghosts exist in two places at once: the physical earth and the spirit world at the same time.

Continue your education as long as you can; it never hurts to get more knowledge. Never stop learning in general, and always be diligent in your studies and desire to grow in wisdom.

God takes care of today, and God will take care of tomorrow if you surrender to Him daily and proclaim His greatness and give Him the praise He deserves.

Rock beats scissors and makes for a great spiritual foundation to build on too.

Don't be fancy and stuck up, for the Lord requires none of these traits.

Be noble in your intentions, and do not get led into temptation.

If you put a woman in ropes and chains in this life, you will be in ropes and chains in the afterlife. Bet on that!

Rock steady.

There are other higher entities and energy frequencies that exist in our world with us. They are usually here for a visit to earth, and they sometimes intervene when there is a call of distress in our lives. They are allowed to help humans in need, for that is the case. There are also lower-frequency beings that are immature and cause mischievous dealings with humans as well. Some call them demons, but sometimes they are just immature spirits who have mischievous ways still and are not developed for proper loving.

Sometimes, we need vacations from ourselves, but we can never avoid responsibility completely. We need responsibility to grow, and it's a part of our goal here on earth to complete certain tasks, so don't disappear for too long; there's a lot to do.

Take your time deciding who to give your love to; it's a serious decision, and you must have the heart of a turtle.

Love is patiently watching your child play in the ocean during the setting sun over the ocean.

Remember to return to the sea at least once a year to regain spiritual focus and to complete the cycle of life once again.

The words of a father hold great influence on a man's children. The father must choose his words and actions carefully, for they will be repeated and reenacted in the mouths and actions of his children as they learn and yearn to follow him as they grow up. The apple doesn't fall far from the tree.

The sins of the father are imprinted and influence his children's personality traits.

True forgiveness and gentle love can trump and conquer every bad emotion that existed before.

Special needs in a child should not be masked with useless psych drugs.

A child with special needs needs a father and mother with special love.

If there was a twelfth commandment, it would be, "Honor thy children."

Joy exists on a grand scale when looking at a child at play.

Joy is the growth of a child's spirituality and seeing it manifest.

Make every day a special day for the sake of your children's love development. Try and give them their every desire within reason. To do this is a blessing of grand proportion.

Angels and parents guard the hearts of innocent children so that they can grow up without wicked intentions or desires or be influenced by bad ones.

For those who are cursed and have no children, try and spend some time with a family member's child so that you don't miss out on the many blessings they hold.

Being with the favor of a child that is not yours will be a major catalyst to go have some of your own someday.

Children are more precious than the New York City skyline.

A child should never have to grow up with only one parent around. This is a love crime.

September 11 still exists and is remembered on a daily basis by those who have suffered great loss and by those who have found the love of God's greatness. Never forget all the actions and miracles that God performed on that mighty day on such a grand scale. God showed up that morning and was working harder than ever.

Love can be found in the sharing of food.

You know you have a good friend if you can trust them to use your cell phone without being sneaky or malicious.

God had a plan for you before you were even born on earth.

If you truly love someone, you will always hold forgiveness in your heart for them every time they slip up and do you wrong.

Remember to eat and become full of energy, but you can energize from fasting as well.

Here is a four-letter word that can bring you greatness: love.

Your spirit becomes baptized every time you jump into the ocean, for the ocean is considered to be holy water without limits and form. The ocean is sacred water.

Sometimes, angels or deceased family members will take over a child's body to speak or sing through their mouths. Pay close attention to their words and what the message is. Learn to recognize when this happens. Usually, when you ask the child what he was just saying or singing, he usually won't and can't remember what it was. That is just one good indicator.

"He sees you everywhere all the time." These are the glorious lyrics to a children's song sung by Gabriel Blue.

There are so many blessings that come from being a parent that you can't count that high.

Having children keeps you seeing the world as being young at heart. If you do this, you may inherit the kingdom of heaven with ease.

To become a godfather holds great significance and is a great honor. There are many blessings ahead of you if you uphold your obligation.

If you're trying to teach a lesson, at least have a clear and precise point of view or else you are just fumbling around with vain words.

Proverbs

If, after all your good deeds are done, you are still a liar and a cheat, then you are still just a liar and a cheat.

When you deserve blessings, they flow to you like hotcakes. When you don't deserve blessings, you're still just a sinner.

You can have two wives, that is, if you can tell both of them the truth and have them still believe and put love into you, and if you can handle two times the affection, not to mention all the energy you'll spend on trying to balance the equation between the two of them and their needs, which can be a daunting deed. Go ahead had two. King David had eight, and King Solomon had seven hundred of them.

What's in our nature is there for a reason, and there's only so long you can suppress the true desires of your affections. Stay true to yourself, and you will never fall, but seek balance and harmony within your dualities and conflicting actions.

When you feel the Holy Spirit, your whole body begins to vibrate on a high frequency, and when you're chasing the blues, you are stuck on a lower frequency like a slug.

When you tell one lie, it leads to another one, and then another one, and then some more.

Being caught between two different women's love can be more trying and reckless than taking place in a car-smashing derby.

Time seems to disappear, and freedom dies when you're living a lie on both ends of the burning love candle.

You will never find a happy place when you are splitting your love in half between two different lovers.

Being in love with two women never ends with an "I love you."

You deserve only the finest of God's blessings, but when you aren't in compliance with the correct laws of nature, you might get hit with a whammy or two instead. So don't cry when it happens.

God wrote the Book of Love, and in it, there isn't a section that says it's okay to be a cheater and a liar.

When you invest your time and energy into cultivating a mass quantity of love in some fashion, you do not want to sever from all the hard work you put into it, but you want to let it fly free from judgment and the depths of sorrow and failure. Invest with wisdom, and your love shall flourish.

Someone may use fancy words to get out of a sticky situation, but fancy is boisterously full of ignorance and greed.

You can never really block a woman in scorn; she will find a way to be heard and feared.

How many risks can one man really take when he's looking down a spiritual double-barreled shotgun of a woman in scorn?

It's one thing to mend a broken heart with a game of hearts, but it's another thing to be the Jack of Hearts breaking hearts.

Consider the truth a spiritual obligation, and don't slack on it.

It is possible to feel love and hate at the same time, but there is still hate, and it cancels out the good.

Some people can't accept the truths of the reality they live in, so they lie, cheat, and steal any which way but lose.

Those who hide behind religion when they are ravenous wolves are hypocrites and can't be trusted. They are usually the loudest ones in the pack who boast about so-called blessings.

Gentle love can be beaten down and ruined by even the smallest of lies.

You know you're in trouble when you request an eagle grip for yourself.

Everything will be okay when you repent and tell the truth to the victims you hurt.

Salvation can be obtained by planting good seeds and ripping off the tares to be burnt in the fire.

Whenever there is a disagreement of actions that took place, go back and double and triple check your facts and information to ensure you're in the clear and your hands are washed of any guilt.

The more noble you think you are, the greater God will test your will and character.

Either you're walking with Jesus, or you're running with the devil. The choice is yours; God gave us free will.

Suffering from acid eye is a form of spiritual blindness.

There are never two winners at the racetrack, but only one becomes victorious.

The shame doesn't usually settle in until there is clarity of the mind.

Lying to your lover is like burning up upon the earth's atmosphere upon reentry from outer space.

A day of joy can easily turn into a day of suffering something awful when you're lying to yourself about the absolute truths at hand. You will most likely be doing an activity that is pointless and getting nowhere fast because you're fighting the actions the whole way through because of your chronic dissatisfaction with the event and person you're partaking in with. Sometimes, we must go backward before we can go forward.

Make an effort not to punish yourself for your iniquities, for you would not commit them if life wasn't a trial-and-error situation that eventually leads to becoming wiser in the end. We are not perfect.

When it's time for action and to come clean about your sinful nature, don't beat around the bush for an easy way out.

To steal sleep and dreams away from yourself is an act of pure foolishness. Sometimes, you have to just quit while you are behind and call it a night.

Jesus died for your sins and there's such a gift as holy communion, so rejoice, your sins can be forgiven.

Don't beat yourself to death over such trivial things as text message lovers, for a telephone call is worth more than a million written words in jest.

Nothing lasts forever when you are spiritually rolling dice and shooting craps. Don't play a game of chance that is structured for you to lose everything including your faith.

The worth of your love can be measured by the number of scars on your heart.

Your morals will always be in conflict with what's considered having a good time.

If you can't come correct, you shouldn't be allowed to come at all.

True peace is but a momentary feeling; embrace it while it lasts, for it's always in conflict with monumental suffering on earth.

No more suffering on earth is the goal.

Don't count on happiness to save the day when you're crossing the lines of wickedness in the river of filth.

When we die, our souls can go to a non-spiritual place, much like a complete black purgatory that we build for ourselves if we are unhappy with our actions while we are alive on earth. You will remain there for many seasons to come.

Stare into your eyes in the mirror. Are they hungry, or are they satisfied? And ask yourself how you got here. It is important to recognize the patterns of how we got there in the first place and what we are still searching for.

There is much heat and destruction when you're texting with a fire heart emoji.

Please be kind to yourself and forgive yourself with ease because guilt can pile up so quickly to become a demon-feeding frenzy filled with shame and humility.

When you love someone, you do twice the suffering.

Never take for granted the freedoms you have been given, for your story can change with the snap of God's fingers if He is unhappy with your actions or motives.

At the center core of our hearts lays an instinctual goodness of human nature but sometimes it's covered with the sins of our pleasures, and we must pray to wash them away in order to shine again.

Tell yourself it's okay because everything is exactly where it needs to be, and you're right on track for your next great move toward holiness.

You hold the keys to your own destiny. Are they speedy access slip-in cards, or are they old-fashioned metal keys that take a little finessing to open doors?

You can't always get what you want, for you must make precise decisions that sometimes encompass the less and unwanted but correct pathway to success. And that's just a fact of life. Suck it up.

Never be ashamed of the mess you made because you made it in the quest for true love.

Every time you write something down, you establish a written contract with the words you have chosen.

Always try and look at life through the best-case scenario syndrome filter.

Doctors and therapists are always judging character and are quickly willing to put an element and negative title on your image and personality. They don't realize it, but they are really cursing you with their titles and classifications and limiting your own personal growth. For example, many doctors said that Bruce Lee would never walk again after becoming quadriplegic. And not only did he walk again but he became the greatest kung fu fighter in the world. Think of what he would have become if he listened to all the doctors. There is a power in the will of the mind to overcome any title or obstacle, especially if you have God's favor. Everybody's bipolar now; what does that even mean? It's just another limiting title that holds you back from greatness and mental health. Pay no mind. We shall overcome.

Feel empathy for those trapped in the confines of a negative marriage. Trying to keep a family connected should be the main priority, but in some cases, a separation is definitely needed to continue a mentally and physically healthy relationship for all future dealings. But if you had God on your side, it wouldn't have been an issue from the start. Seriously.

I love turning frowns upside down. Usually, this can be achieved with some gentle love or some brief comical relief. Try both methods in trying to cheer someone up.

Don't get caught like a deer in headlights; plan for the unexpected.

Don't journey near dangerous human beings who drive and act irrationally while in a moving motor vehicle.

Bearing false witness is like having a head-on car crash with a giant fire truck with its sirens blasting and with its lights flashing.

"Thou shalt not bear false witness against thy neighbour" (Exodus 20:16). This is one of the Ten Commandments.

When you repent, God opens your river so that everyone afflicted by your behavior can hear your sins and confession. Even the devil hears you and awaits to devour you. Repenting is far from a private affair between you and God, so be prepared to tell the world what you have done. But don't worry, and stay calm, cool, and collected because you will usually find forgiveness in the end.

The Lord's mercies are great when we confess our sins out loud and pray for forgiveness.

If I am wrong, correct me. If I am right, then thank me. For if I am right and wrong, I'm still wrong.

There is no sickness or distress or wickedness when one's basking in the everlasting white light that comes from the Lord and His throne. Its presence sustains all things and brings peace and order to the kingdom of heaven. It's so beautiful there isn't a word on earth to describe it. Some call it "The Presence."

Once you've worked something out, always go back and double- and triple-check your efforts and find a new way to make it even better. If it needs no reworking, then it's a minimal blessing, and you should stop in your tracks right away and not add another thing to it. Congrats, you did it, but usually, you can find at least one other element to add to it to bring the piece of work to a higher dimensional state of existence. For example, I do a painting, and I glue a stick a certain way onto the canvas to bring it to a higher state of being. The painting might have been fine and stayed minimal with just the paint, but now the wood adds another dimension to its purpose and meaning by putting a piece of nature onto it. Usually, the less is better, but try and find things to multiply its meaning and power.

Falling asleep and dreaming about a woman you know and desire is always a treat, but sometimes it can be a demonic mimic tricking and luring you into temptation. So, try to abstain from having sexual relations in dreams and curb your fleshly desires. The dream state is the spirit world manifested, and you should think and act in a spiritual manner when you're having a vision, no matter how insignificant the dream may be. God watches our actions even in our dreams. So, try and come correct in this asleep state of mind. What happens in the dream world affects our daily world and behaviors too. The two worlds feed off each other.

Try and work with God when you're dreaming a dream. He is always watching you, beholding the good and the evil. He wants to see what you can create and bring to the table for His glory. Whom art.

Jesus said, "I came not to send peace, but a sword" (Matthew 10:34).

There's nothing like the joy of actually talking to a real old friend whom you haven't seen in a while and just spending a day or two catching up and reminiscing about old stories and the glorious conquests of your travels.

Happiness is sharing a fire or two with a passionate lover or crony.

Happy are those who wear Jesus' Band-Aid across their hearts and souls. You can get some on eBay for pretty cheap if you need some. They are twice as healing as a normal Band-Aid. This is the truth.

Building idols is like stepping into a pile of doggie doodie and getting it stuck deep down in the carpet and the ridges of your brand-new sneakers.

Don't be sorry until you feel sick of the situation and want some resolution on the sins of your doings. Then be very sorry.

Be prepared to pay for the future wrongdoings before they even manifest. You may or may not stop the sin from happening, but at least you're preparing to be responsible for your actions and the consequences that shall apply.

Take control of your destiny and settle for nothing less than what you want and deserve.

Make sure you are always caught up in your sleep; your heart will thank you for caring.

Don't lie to get money out of somebody; this will make that money dirty and cursed, so bad things will end up coming from it.

Some thieves' codes are based strictly on karma, and they won't steal from you until you sin first. This then justifies them to rob you, so they won't feel any guilt or shame about their devious actions. They also know that God doesn't protect the sinner, which allows them to get away with it. That's why thieves are always looking for a God-fearing man to prey upon.

When trying to accomplish a goal of grand proportion, you need prayers, or you'll never make it.

Where there is sorrow, there is pain; the two go hand in hand.

Broken marriages are twice as nasty when there's a child involved in the middle of the battle for separation. A child needs both his parents to ensure success. Make the right plans to ensure that both parents will still be in that kid's life after the separation occurs. At least promise to still be there for them somehow. Find a way.

There are generational curses that can be passed down through one's family members. If this applies to you and your family, you all should get deliverance to break the vicious cycle in order to regain the spirit of success again.

You'll never truly appreciate the meaning of being a parent until you try and mentor a child and correct his path. Once you endured the hardships of responsibility, you may then begin to understand what parents go through and the sacrifices it takes to make a happy, loving family. Don't put down parenthood. It's a serious job that needs love and support.

When you build on God's love, you can never fail or lose.

A separation is never needed if you hold God's love in your heart and soul.

Good love is so rare it's like an endangered species. Once you find it you should become it and produce everything you got toward keeping it growing in the right direction.

Good, gentle love should never have to be sacrificed; it stands together and keeps shining forever.

Be the one to say what is in God's plan for those who are sinners and misbehave. When they lose the argument because they don't understand the ways of His laws, have mercy on them, for they know not what they do and put it in God's hands. He always fixes the problem at hand in some way or fashion, and a great lesson will be learned somehow. Sinners heed this caution. You will get dealt with somehow in some way.

When you break the rules and spiritual laws that exist, you are only going to be breaking yourself in the end. You can bet on that.

The truth, when spoken and delivered at the perfect occasion, can be glorious and never refuted. For truth rains over all dark valleys of lies and will conquer the unjust and deceitful time and time again through thick and thin.

When doves cry, they lose water in their tears. When doves fly, they soar in freedom with no fears.

Sometimes, you need deer beers for two. What that means is that it's okay to fill your love with some spirits or new wine once in a while, especially when you're traveling through some thick woods in the impending lure of the shiny moonlit night of romance with your lover. Lovers sometimes get special privileges when love is blossoming.

Suffering stops when love is blossoming.

Have no fear; hold a rock.

Sometimes, we must dance until the break of dawn and give it our all. This can be spiritually important when the flow comes a-calling. Give it your all.

Proverbs

Be like the mighty oak tree; you may lose a branch or two in a vicious storm, but oakwood will remain and constantly be growing toward heaven at a slow and fashionable pace forever.

Try and see the future and paint it a nice positive face for it. And if you don't paint, start doing it; what are you waiting for? Let your imagination run wild.

Your extra efforts will be rewarded. You can double your blessings with a full charge over the hill. Don't be scared either.

When war comes, you will feel it in your bone marrow. When peace comes, your heart flutters gently.

Where there is doubt and despair, your presence is needed. Where there is love and joy, your presence is needed.

To dream of someone more than three times is a special blessing and is not to be overlooked. God's trying to show you something symbolic in nature about yourself by using that person's image again and again. Pay close attention to the little details if you can remember them. These dreams are important.

Never hit or abuse an animal, even if it bites you. It had its reasons for doing so in the first place and does not deserve human retaliations or aggressions which can be cruel and unjust at times.

Pets are so important and special. If you see someone abusing a pet, don't be afraid to report them to the authorities. It's the right thing to do, and you will never get shamed for doing so.

Plants are so important for our peace of mind and spiritual growth. Try to fill every room you have with a plethora of greenness. They can bring warmth and energy into a room that can be so healing for the mind, body, and soul. And they all love it when you play Bob Marley and water them with bong water to grow. This is a strange but true fact.

When someone kisses you, always remember to thank them for

it. One kiss could change your world and cause a revolution in your heart and soul.

Catfishes are the lowest of the low. They're right at the bottom of the barrel, and their love crimes are almost unforgivable.

Where there are sirens, there lay danger.

It's impossible to find peace when they are talking your ears off.

Be careful what you say because the devils have tricks and love to twist your words around and throw them back at you. Be conscious of the words you use. They are like verbal contracts.

Tomorrow is always another day and a fresh beginning to make a change for the better and greater good.

There is only so much ignorance one can listen to. If you are caught in this position, the best thing to do is say "God bless you" and disconnect from the conversation. A fool will talk forever and get nowhere.

Payback for bad karma is a humdinger of an experience. When God is angry, it's Murphy's law sometimes. Change your ways before it's too late.

Losing your life's work on a hard drive can be heartbreaking, but at least you didn't lose your soul or spirituality.

Feeling upset with the way things are working out is part of the growing process. We must strive for success at all costs and never quit. If you have to go backward in order to go forward, then that's what you have to do. Accept the absolute truths, and you'll be a happier person, and you will go much farther, much faster.

Disappointment can burn you to the core; letting go can save you from suffering.

Your entire honor can be erased with the slip of one foul thought that seeps from your lips in a loose conversation with a heathen. Choose your words carefully. Don't say things that would upset Jesus or that go against your own religion. This is a sin.

Too much talk, not enough work. Talk less and produce more.

When someone leaves you no choice but to pray for justice, you must still find mercy and forgiveness in your heart because it goes so much further. Justice only leads to more justice, and what does that solve but put everyone in hot water and stuck in judgment? Mercy frees the soul for healing and offers a better life path choice.

When all is lost, there is God. He's never lost, and you can always find Him with the saying of a simple prayer.

Things break and destroy your heart's works; sometimes, there is nothing you can do but be at the mercy of God so that the problem gets fixed without a hitch or glitch.

When you carry your computer around without a cover and have loose wires dangling from it, it is a direct reflection of your mind's mind and how you carry yourself. So don't be disappointed when your stuff doesn't work right. You did not protect it in the first place, and you were too lazy to cover it properly. This is a direct reflection of your soul's management as well.

Some problems you can fix, and some were meant for disappointment. There is a lesson in either one.

Be satisfied with what you still have to offer the world. Just because you lose some of your personal possessions does not mean you have lost your ideals and dreams. Be grateful for what you have and for what you can bring to the spiritual table.

The password is "Jesus."

Some people love, and some people fight, and some people love to fight.

Tell more stories that end in victory and not sorrow; it's up to you to keep morale up with others.

A sad story has its time and place, usually when we are sharing grief with somebody, or a great lesson shall be taught afterward. But try and avoid them altogether.

Trying to dodge faith and religion is like playing a game of chicken in an automobile.

On 9/11, some men jumped and went to heaven, and some men jumped and went to hell, but there was a moment of repentance and a need for God's help before it was too late. Many prayed at this time, in these trying moments, and found salvation.

It's too late to cry over spoiled spiritual milk, for you had a long time to decide not to drink it.

Clarity can be found when smoking in mass quantities. This is also when you realize that smoking is bad for you.

Fame is a drug that will leave you dissatisfied and empty in the end. How sweet it was.

Don't ever tell Jesus or God to go f*** Himself. This is a serious crime.

Even the greatest super celebrity stars fart and take doo-doos just like you do; we are all humans doing human things, no one's better than the rest.

A woman needs extra love and affection while she's menstruating.

Making peace with a shark in a dream is considered a great accomplishment.

Albino eagles bite the heads of the snakes of wrath.

When you fast, you can starve the spiritual snakes and impurities out of your body if you have any.

Where can you run when a mighty lion has it in for you?

Orcas hold great spiritual power and are very mysterious and beautiful creatures.

A philosopher is a lover of wisdom.

Proverbs

Never be ashamed to wear hand-me-downs, for they come equipped with twice the love.

Follow the gut feelings you get when they arrive in your stomach. Usually, it doesn't lie.

All your sins are duly noted when they are collected at all the borderlines.

The path of a sinner is a hard pill to swallow.

Voices may tell you that some things are good or bad, but it's the voice you have inside the one that really matters. We are responsible for our own happiness, not the happiness of a bunch of critics.

If you don't have forgiveness in your heart, you have an empty heart.

There is no way you can be a good parent from long distances away and only having supervised telephone calls.

Be prepared for the unexpected; be willing to go the extra mile at any given moment. The Lord throws us some trying situations.

The freedom that comes from a motorcycle can be addictive and seriously dangerous.

The imagination can run circles around the absolute truths that exist in a lover's intentions. Try not to get carried away with jealous or selfish visions that don't exist at all. Our imagination can get the best of us sometimes. Imagine with your spiritual eyes instead, and always seek the truth.

When you're stuck on the catfish algorithm, trust no one and get to blocking. Save yourself the time, energy, grief, love, and money. Be strong. Lead us not into temptation.

Evil and wickedness in a child is the parent's fault for not instilling better values and having greater discipline. A stern whooping on the ass for correction when they do something wrong may just save them a lifetime of misery and rebellion, and even drug abuse.

There is a time to play and a time to work. God makes time for both these things.

Children are the ultimate teachers; listen as they evaluate and discuss all their surroundings and findings; usually, they are pretty accurate and extremely blunt.

There are your tidings, and there are your offerings; know the difference. Tidings are what you owe due to a set income that you receive, and offerings are the extra you put in after your tidings that bring abundant blessings into your life for your extra generosity.

Don't get stuck on the spiritual carousel going round and round in the same place, listening to the same things without progress or change.

We must write things down in order to see them manifest. Writing is a declaration and statement that holds great power. It also helps one to reflect on the nature of the writing and its meaning by revisiting it over and over again.

You can't see what's invisible to your human eye unless you open the dormant areas of your brain through stimulants or serious meditations. You may also do this by using both your hands equally in balance with each other, being ambidextrous, which then crosses the brain waves from the right and left side equally to open your brain chakra. Then, the hidden realms are possible to see.

With great vision comes greater responsibility. With greater responsibility comes greater wisdom. With greater wisdom comes easier judgment upon one. With an easier judgment comes the greater possibility of earning eternal, everlasting life.

Being called a pervert can never be a good thing. God doesn't like perverts.

Doing wrong never feels too good. It just feels wrong, and you know it.

Proverbs

You can read the Bible a hundred times, but if you still haven't learned anything and applied it to your life, it means nothing, and you've just wasted your and God's time.

You can go to church a hundred times, but if you still go out into the world and do worldly things and sin a lot, then what's the point of even going? You're just making God angry with your foolishness and wasting everybody's precious time. Have you learned nothing?

Be on your best behavior twenty-four hours a day, seven days a week.

When the work is over, you will know it's time to quit, but if the work isn't done yet, you must burn the candle at both ends in order to stay on track with your personal goals. Time is so short here on earth. Live and let live, and definitely work harder.

Remembering to keep the Sabbath holy means getting a lot of rest. But if you're a priest, your work is doubled on the Sabbath. He must rest later in the day after the work is done.

Try to never drive another man's car but your own.

Jesus said all you must do is to think about it in your heart, and the deed is done. So be careful what you think. Angels can read your mind and then record these ponderings in a book.

There is nothing in this world that is hidden and not seen. All is revealed in due time as well.

Saying you're sorry just doesn't cut it sometimes; you must hold deep regret in the core of your heart and truly repent for the hideous sins you've committed with a guilty and surrendering demeanor. If you're not feeling it, how do you expect God to?

Masturbating is a vain act and not considered to be spiritual.

Recognize the ultimate truths behind your objectives and never lie about what you're doing to achieve them.

Spiritual blinders are placed over the head of the sinner by demons when he's in sin in order to stop him from seeing holiness and making the correct choices he needs to see to get him out of the current state he is in. This can be disastrous to him spiritually. Be conscious of the blinders.

When you can't recognize yourself in the mirror, you know you have a spiritual problem on your hands that needs immediate attention. Pray without ceasing.

Trouble can find you if you're looking for it.

Doomed love is no longer considered romantic.

Get off the phone before you get into a car crash or, even worse, bump into a catfish or scam artist.

You can't impress those who have no respect for creation; stop trying so hard to win their affection. It's as useless as a tit on a bore.

Pink is sexy by nature and is reserved for those with exotic tastes.

The world will be here waiting when you get back from healing yourself, so don't rush.

"Holy" means "dedicated or consecrated to God or a religious purpose."[1] Holy is sacred.

If you mess with the bull, you're going to get the horns or get stampeded to death. Stop messing around now before you regret ever meeting such a creature.

Try not to become a kundalini enthusiast because it's just a very dangerous serpent power that most end up abusing or falling victim to it because they are not skilled in such arts. Plus, serpent worship is considered forbidden and unholy by the Lord.

Surround yourself with artistic people; it is with them that you will begin to flourish in a positive direction in your quest for the unknown and self-reflection.

Surround yourself with church people, for it is with them that

---

[1] Definition from Oxford Languages.

you will be free from worldly wants and sinful deeds. Your church family will not let you fall or ever wrong you in some fashion.

Kicking a drug habit will be almost impossible without the help of a higher power such as God and Jesus. They have the authority and power to cure your sickness with a snap of a finger. Pray without ceasing, for you need God's love when getting off hard drugs.

Here are three words of wisdom that guarantee you success in all your dealings: "Pray without ceasing" (1 Thessalonians 5:17).

I've never heard of a transgender rock because nobody knows the true sexes of a rock anyway.

Channeling someone's thoughts is more prevalent than you think. Whenever you're off-topic and saying things that you normally don't say, it's usually a sign that your energy is crossing the wave frequencies of another person you know or do not know, and you're picking up their thoughts that manifest through your words and actions. It can come from a soul guide, a spirit, a lost or immature spirit, a lost lover, an animal, or a real human being right on earth. It all depends upon what you said and your ability to know that it manifested from someone else. So always be on the lookout for such occurrences because they're more frequent than you think. Knowing of these special occurrences gives you strength in the spirit realms and an advantage. Not that it's a competition, but it's just a helpful and a very unique tool to be aware of and have in your spiritual belt.

The more you know about how evil works, the better you will become at avoiding it, but innocence is bliss and has its rewards as well. It's a "what you don't know won't hurt you" type of deal, and in some cases, you're really better off not knowing how true evil manifests to begin with so that it won't manifest just by thinking about it.

Be careful of a woman who calls herself a good witch. She still practices witchcraft.

"You get old too soon and smart too late" (John Wislocky).

Don't be afraid to try and conquer love again after the abuses of a previous relationship. How do you think we heal from that anyway? Try, try again, and next time, just be wiser in your selection process.

Sometimes, people fight because their love is too great to be offended, and they won't stand to be insulted or disrespected for another minute. It is important not to return to the same argument that you have had previously over and over again and again. That is a dead-end vicious cycle full of unforgiveness and betrayal that goes nowhere fast. Keep it fresh and to current topics because that's where you are at the moment. You're not living in the past, and it serves no purpose to go there again and again. That is backward thinking. Focus on the problem at hand and how to solve it ASAP. That is positive thinking.

There are many lessons to learn when you have the desire to learn them.

There is nothing you can do to stop the history that has already been written for you. It's in the stars at this point. You might as well make a wish to try and change your destiny.

You can hear the breathing of an angry woman miles away before she's even in your soul's path.

The lessons and hardships one must endure during a lifetime of suffering are mind-bending to think about. But what you can think about is how many joys you've manifested to overcome all the sufferings you've had.

The Lord works in mysterious ways. He can turn a sworn enemy into a best friend. This is just one way God can bless you.

Proverbs

"When a man's ways please the Lord, he maketh even his enemies to be at peace with him" (Proverbs 16:7).

A sworn female enemy can be turned into a faithful lover under the right circumstances. The soul has a plan of its own for you and the one you're going to give your love to. It's out of your control. If it was meant to happen, it shall happen. This was written years ago, before your birth, in a controlled viewing room of destiny. Sometimes opposites attract, and a greater lesson of love is learned. God had a plan for you from the start; consider it a blessing when this mating ritual occurs because it's so rare and so beautiful.

Don't drift off into some wild and obscene sexual fantasy; stay focused on the mission, which is to have a true, gentle lover to hold and cherish from here to eternity. Your soulmate will find you soon enough in this crazy world we live in. Just don't let her go when you finally find her.

You can get reincarnated as some alien on a foreign planet somewhere in the universe to live out a life or two to learn some lesson, but this is unrewarding because most aliens do not possess the ability to laugh, and that is important for our spiritual growth. Choose earth. Earth is the place where dreams come true, and the soul flourishes.

There is nothing more stifling than the spirit of money and its burden on the people of the earth. We try to break free from its curse by obtaining more of it, but it only adds to the problem. The more money you have, the bigger your problems will be. Plus, God will be testing your character along the way many times, and you can bet on that.

Doing wickedness is like being strapped down inside of a monster truck passenger seat while flying over and smashing other cars in its path of destruction.

Love comes easy when you're walking to please thee.

The Joker will never ever beat Batman, no matter how hard he tries and no matter how many diabolical schemes he pulls and no matter how many bad jokes he tells.

The criminal mind is stupid and greedy and doesn't know when to quit. They get caught because they get sloppy, and it's only a matter of time before God gives them what they deserve anyway. So have patience if you are involved with criminals and their activities; they'll definitely get theirs. I promise you that.

Never let the amount of money one has determine your friends.

Wicked imaginations kill the soul, too; you don't even need to act upon it; just thinking is bad enough.

Cheaters will stop at nothing to try and get what they want; some may have to get busted a ton of times before they mend their ways. It's in their nature to cheat. But it is also in our nature to be truthful and honest as well. Being honest is always more rewarding.

Praying all together with members of your church is such a powerful way to pray. There is great strength when we come together in unison under God's roof. Strength enough to change the world.

It takes courage to be the only one telling the truth. Numerous people seem to believe in and live in lies most of the time, and they will hate you for pointing it out to them.

I feel sorry for the people who believe in God but don't read the Scripture or go to church or sacrifice and spend any time with Him. How do they expect to grow? They want to reap the benefits of having a loving God without ever really giving praise or worship to Him. They might as well believe in the Easter Bunny too.

The Easter Bunny is a false idol that the devil uses in order to take away the true meaning of Easter, which is Christ getting crucified and then rising from the dead after three days, becoming an ultimate sacrifice for the sins of mankind, not hidden bunny eggs with chocolate and jelly beans.

Dreams with your parents or grandparents are very sacred and special, and you should pay close attention to what happens, for there is always a deeper message in these dreams. It can also be their souls talking to you directly if they have already passed away. Pray for these types of dreams, and they will come more frequently.

No one is really dead unless they are stuck in hell or a personal purgatory of some sort that they have created for themselves. Then they're not allowed to reach you at the current time.

I wish the devil was not real, but he is. So, suck it up and stop your sinning.

Many evil people on earth who commit serious crimes and do dark magic and have sold their souls become the devil's slaves in the afterlife, left to do his bidding for eternity. They try to possess, haunt, and kill human beings who are still alive. If they don't do their job and take more souls to hell, which is their main goal, they will ultimately suffer even greater punishment for their failures and be seriously tortured as well. They become demon slaves.

Committing suicide is one of the most selfish acts a person can ever do and is not looked favorably by God. It could earn you a trip to hell in most cases, so don't attempt such a stupid act. But there have been cases where the person has made it to heaven as well. This is the truth.

The only thing you should fear is losing God's grace and love. Then, you are screwed.

God tests our faith, hope, and love in times when we are in trouble. Never lose any of these elements because they are all around and exist in everything. It's all about your perspective, and God wants to see our loyalty and courage to test our will of character. This was a test that most people fail, but His good servant Job didn't. Try to hold the super faith, super hope, and super love that Job did, and your troubles shall flee from you, and blessings shall blossom in its place.

Let Jesus become your Boaz.

We are what we believe, and we are what God made us to be as well.

The enemy can never take you as long as your sins are covered. If they aren't covered, you are more prone and acceptable to illness and torment by unholy principalities. When you are covered, even the weak parts of your body remain strong, like you have a protective seal over you. When you're not covered, you shall feel every ache and pain and become spiritually emptied like a rusty, hallowed tin can.

Feel sorry for those who say f* God this and f* Jesus that! For they just have never known or experienced the complete power of what a gentle love brings. Pray for them.

Hope and pray to God that you never have to learn what a trial by fire means.

Love is becoming; it suits everyone everywhere and consumes everything.

Since Adam and Eve covered themselves, then so should we.

Nudist colonies aren't free from being nude.

There is much to learn about oneself when writing a personal list of proverbs. Try it sometime. The process is rewarding and carries many blessings.

There is much to gain from avoiding rash decisions; never do anything when you're rushed. Take a turtle's time when deciding something important.

There are many blessings from hearing a child praying. It's more precious than a king's entire kingdom and all his riches. Get your kid into active prayer from an early age.

Families that pray together stay together.

People who take the Lord's name in vain all the time are just cursing themselves. This is a no-no.

When everything you do is a lose-lose situation, you have to get deliverance from the spirit of failure.

Taking holy communion washes away our sins and brings forth the Holy Spirit to work within us.

If a thief wants something so bad, then let him have it, for no crime goes unpunished, and he'll get his punishment in the end anyway, so don't feel too bad about what was lost. Don't put yourself in more danger by trying to be the hero. Pray for his salvation.

The mass smash-and-grab acts that are constantly taking place in California now are the works of a legion of demons controlling a desperate group or gang. That's behavior they do in hell too. They'll even steal from each other when they get the chance too. Nothing is sacred, and everything is greed, greed, greed, and more selfishness. Watch as they'll start to copycat across the country now, much like the school shooting did from watching the Columbine tragedy. Demons work in patterns as well.

The burning of the Woodstock rock festival was the beginning of the end. The future is in mobs herding like flocks of sheep without a GOoD shepherd.

Alien slaves built Egypt.

When God opens the door to your heart and gives you a good woman to love, one who has integrity and a superb moral code, you better respect that gift and treat her right. Try with all your might to keep her and the flame of passion burning for as long as possible.

True love exists, and you are worthy of it. Don't self-sabotage the best thing that could have ever happened to you in your entire life. It's time to put on your Sunday best attitude and become a grown adult. You now are responsible for two hearts and you're now the keeper of the dream. Don't blow it.

With the union of a long-lost soulmate coming into your life, so does the lifting of wretched curses, and this is a cause for celebration, for you now have an abundance of blessings. You will drink from the fountain of youth.

Every king needs a good queen behind him with a loving and loyal attitude. If she possesses these two traits, their kingdom, love, and loyalty shall flourish, and they will establish it with righteousness.

Be everything and then some in the heart of your lover. Go the extra mile to see her smile.

There are queens that come from the county of kings.

When your identity has been stolen, then you'll be sorry.

Now is the time to move right in and conquer the world; now is your window of opportunity; seize the moment, don't be timid, kill the weakest, eat more meat, and become the albino lion. But slow your roll, keep it steady, build the foundation, have patient determination, take your time, easy breezy, eat healthy greens, become the albino turtle. Become the albino lion or the albino turtle, or become them both.

Your soul is like an endless sparkler when it's around its mate.

In order to form a perfect union with your lover, you must possess these seven key ideals: faith, hope, love, patience, understanding, loyalty, and forgiveness. With unity and respect for these elements in your relationship, you can conquer the world and achieve all your desired dreams.

Keeping love alive is a daily occupation.

Proverbs

Sharing your thoughts and dreams with a lover is such a sacred thing to do that when they're properly received, you instantly become blessed by the bond you share together in unison. Sharing is caring.

Take notice how the whole world seems to stop when you're in love. This is the secret to eternal youth.

You may become consumed with love for your soulmate and want them all the time, but don't forget to put the Lord above all first. Then your love shall prosper.

Good dreams bring you closer to God and make the world go round for the entire day. Bad dreams stop your connection to God, rain terror, and ruin your day, which is their main objective. Rebuke these dreams with quickness upon waking up so that you may return to a holy state of mind so that you can save your day from being a total disaster.

"For God so loved the world, that he gave his only begotten Son, that whosoever believeth in him should not perish, but have everlasting life" (John 3:16).

Love is contagious when you are around it.

Faith is precious, like a refined diamond after the coal.

Hope can be found while lying in the arms of a special lover.

Loyalty is like getting a bear hug from an albino grizzly.

Forgiveness comes easy when your love is deep, like a yellow submarine in an octopus's garden.

Understanding one another's nature completely is necessary to merge into a higher state of consciousness.

God supports those who help themselves, and He likes to see you make the first effort to begin with.

These three simple words can change the world: "Love one another."

Hope remains to be seen in everything green.

Love is like the fire from the engine of a rocket ship. It's explosive. It brings you up and up and up and up till you break through all barriers known to exist.

Church bells ring for you. So, listen up for those who have ears.

A good DJ will always help the lesser DJ to evolve, by showing him the ropes on the decks and by giving him gifts of some good vinyl to help grow his collection. He does this with a happy heart and patient mind. He becomes a teacher of trade, which is just another blessing upon blessing.

Light lies in the hearts of those who are saved.

Jesus is like a white diamond dove flying over a highway of speeding cars for all to see.

You must have peace with God to have peace for yourself.

"G" stands for "giving," "great," "good," "grandfather," and "God."

Work until you see double, then rest for a while, then work again. Hard work has its rewards.

Put your love on display so that you can influence the masses.

With great love comes a great responsibility.

Children aren't as naive as you think, they are actually very perceptive and soak in even the littlest of details.

People tend to forget about all the little things that go into making something special. Never forget all the little things. Cherish them.

Don't tell too many jokes. They may rot your soul.

You should never open your relationship sexually with other people with your spouse. Someone always gets hurt in the end.

Divorce is never justified if you have God.

Don't get too old and set in your ways; always try to do things a little differently than what you're used to. Evolve.

If you cheated on your lover once, it's highly likely that you'll do it again. We are creatures of habit.

What's funny is funny, and what's not funny shouldn't be said.

When you live on the edge, you have edgy things happen to you.

You can't squeeze ten pounds of fat out of a five-pound chicken.

Spirits sometimes lie; be careful who you trust, especially if they have nobody.

To hear or not to hear, that is the question. Sometimes, you must hear things you do not want to hear. You're better off not hearing it because once you hear it, you will then be responsible for its meaning and worth.

Make your burden easy and free-flowing like water traveling downstream in no order. Whatever brings you more happiness, just do it, and be satisfied with your actions. If you aren't satisfied, then your burden becomes heavy.

It's not true love if you get jealous. And it's not true love to put your lover in a position where he would get jealous, either.

Some people would give their best horse to obtain a nickname from a *winkte*.

A poor self-image can't help you find love because you don't love yourself. You should love yourself just the way you are.

When you're in love, it's all about trust; without trust, you have nothing.

Don't ever settle for less than what you want, or you will never be happy. Our God is the God of big things, and He will make it all possible for you to reach if that's what's in your heart.

Have an eagle's eye when looking for signs, symbols, and spiritual connections everywhere you go.

Only true, gentle love can mend a broken heart.

To do anything, you must first have God's approval. Without

Him signing off on the deal, you might as well throw in the towel.

There comes a point in suffering when you cannot suffer anymore; there's only one way to go from there, and that is up, up, up.

On the path to truth and honor and halo rings, there are many tests. You must pray to pass them all.

Let the fire of love's light burn with no end in sight. Do not get detoured by the winds of the past to blow it out. Keep a mighty flame and let it shine, shine, shine, for the sake of love.

But will you take thee in sickness and in health, for better or worse? Because that's true love.

Try and be healthy for your lover, and do not present yourself as a slob or messy person.

When all you have isn't good enough, it's time for life life-changing experience, and you better change fast before you lose what blessings could be coming to you.

Forgive us, for we are man; forgiveness as the numbers of sands.

To catch a shooting star, you must be flying just as fast as it.

When you're dating someone, you might as well be dating all their friends, too, because you're going to have to live up to their standards as well. Without their approval, your relationship will go nowhere as well.

You don't need someone to tell you you're doing the wrong thing; you already know.

Don't waste all your creative talents making art for the person who you know doesn't know how to respect it. You might as well give them your heart on a platter to eat.

When something is over, end it. Don't keep returning to it like when you keep poking a wound because it feels like a good pain. It's still a pain, and you should leave it alone.

Strawberries are known to be a fruit of passion.

Proverbs

Just remember that when you're on top, there will always be a willingness to chop you down to steal your spot. Recognize the hater and be prepared for his actions.

There is always something to talk about. You should never be without something to say to someone. If the conversation becomes stale, you have to look at what you're contributing and then make it happen to keep up relations.

When love comes to town, you better get down.

A loyal wife is worth more than all the diamond rings in the world.

When you find a woman who quotes scriptures from the Bible to you, you know you have a winner, and you should marry this woman; she will have your best interests.

Romance is not dead nor hopeless, for it lives and breathes in your every breath. Recognize the potential for it in everything that you do, and you will find it's been there all along from the start. Manifest it in spirit, and it shall bless you with its secrets.

To be in love can be a dangerous thing when your super love emotions rule your actions. Give 120 percent of your love, and if your lover comes back with 120 percent, then you're safe; otherwise, be cautious; someone's bound to get hurt because of heavy expectations.

A soulmate is a person ideally suited to another as a close friend or romantic partner.[2] It's all that and more. It is almost indescribable because the words for such a passionate person don't exist on earth at this present time. Only in heaven is there such an understanding of this natural phenomenon.

Once you find what you've been looking for, will your quest end there? Will you be satisfied with life then? Or will you have

---

2 Definition from *Oxford Dictionary*.

other new quests to conquer? How much do you really need and want? Ask yourself these questions, and if you find your answer, then you've found true love. What more do you need?

When you find the person who finishes your sentences before you think them, you've found a true spiritual partner. Embrace this gift from God.

Just remember that the second you cheat on a lover, God will not bless your union anymore with that person, and He will take it all away from you. The Lord giveth and taketh.

Sometimes, saying nothing can say a thousand words.

Become the turtle in the race for true love; patience is key.

If you are high or drunk, your words are just as important as if you were sober-minded, and words still carry the same meanings. Watch your tongue.

Just don't pray for a piece of the pie; pray for the whole pie. Our God is a God of abundance, and He is the best gift giver in the world. You just must be deserving of it and behold a super faith in the Lord and His greatness. Then you shall have what your heart desires.

It's okay to fall short because then you learn what it must take to become tall.

Never underestimate the power of love and what it can bring if you possess it. Some take years to find it, but once you find it, you can accomplish anything and everything in front of you. True love is the power of God; find Him now.

When two souls melt together in perfect unison, it makes for one unstoppable force to be reckoned with.

Never forget your roots or what it took for you to get where you currently are in life. Reflecting and respecting the past is essential for future growth and successful ventures into the unknown.

Our time is but a breath on earth and can go so shortly, so use it wisely and don't dally when it comes to making the correct decisions the first time around. Conserve your time and energy because time is one thing you can never get back.

When it rains in the valley of death, you know there is a great triumph for the forces of good and the person it's raining for.

When Jesus says, "They'll be none of that," all shall cease, and evil shall scatter back to the hellish depths in which it came from. Jesus doesn't play around. His words are a law to be followed by all forms of life and principalities.

How many conversations can you have before you find the answers? The quest to find love may seem endless sometimes. Have faith. Pray for love, and you shall find it.

When someone shares music with you, they are giving you a piece of their soul's puzzle. Respect the gifts and find the missing piece to their soul through love and devotion.

True love is wanting to care through sickness and health and through the good and the bad times as well.

Nothing can compare to the joy and inspiration one gets from finding true love. It's so rare, like catching a snow leopard's photograph when he climbs to the top of the mountain.

True love is when you live every breath you take for the affection of a worthy lover.

The antichrist can come in many forms, so beware and recognize their bad habits.

Coming into a relationship with a lover who you consider to be your soulmate should run smoothly like a well-greased oiled machine. No problems, and full steam ahead. If it isn't this easy, it's not true love and probably your soul mismatch. So try and try again. The search goes on. Just do yourself a favor and learn from your mistakes so you don't repeat the same relationship over and over again. It's okay to have higher standards when trying to find your true love. Don't settle for less than the best. You deserve more.

Praying for those who are less fortunate than you is an obligation, and you should pray without ceasing so that you can possibly change their outcome. Prayers do get answered.

Have a heart, give, and care more.

Sometimes, two people can't find love no matter what they do to try and obtain it. They either end up fighting or looking for it elsewhere, and in either case, the relationship is doomed. True love will never fight or have lustful eyes. It will always have an understanding of God and the greater good for each other's needs and wants. True love finds a way, no matter what, through having a great faith in God and each other.

Don't be too frugal with your wealth; always give to the needy and less fortunate. You will have your reward for doing this.

There is nothing more beautiful than when two lovers come together in agreement about God's love and His values. They shall have their blessings and become fruitful in unison.

Planting a good seed can be as simple as making a telephone voice connection with the ones you love.

When you find what you have been looking for your entire life, you hold on to it and pray for dear life to keep receiving its blessings.

There is nothing that is hidden in true love; everything is opened to be honored and loved correctly without judgment or malice.

Take out the positive from all situations and leave the negative in the dust where it belongs.

When two souls grow together on the same path, the journey is twice as rewarding. Finding common ground can help elevate your

Proverbs

growth potential too.

Remember to always help the little fish because you were once little yourself before you grew mighty. Always pay it back.

You can never repeat the phrase "I love you" too many times. It's always needed and should always be welcomed.

Try and set at least two hours a day to connect to the Lord somehow, and you will prosper greatly.

Until you have the Bible memorized, you should keep reading it daily.

Patience in love is an understatement and should not go undercooked.

Whatever brings you the maximum quantity of joy and happiness should be cherished and pursued, as long as it doesn't defy the laws of the Lord, of course.

Stand for something good and take a just and noble position. Don't be lukewarm in your dealings or follow the ways of a fool.

Foolish behaviors can always be found in young and precocious love.

Wisdom is like having the perfect tool for the job at hand.

You are either growing in an upward or downward direction; there is no middle highway route of balance.

God wrote the Bible.

God appreciates sobriety and deems it a righteous way of living.

No matter how much good you do, if you fail to comply with the Lord's laws, you're just always going to be another sinner praying for salvation.

Do not make false accusations about a neighbor or enemy, for this is a sin. Always tell the truth.

The truth will never be hidden from those who seek it. It has a way of being clairvoyant and noticeable for all who search for its validity.

What brings you happiness and is considered joyful by nature can be diminished and diluted in seconds by the actions of a drunken fool.

Never stop the quest for true freedom, and be valiant in your efforts to obtain it.

Don't say you're sorry if you're not; it only makes you look ignorant and foolish.

You can move a giant boulder with the proper use of your faith and determination.

Never quit what brings you happiness; happiness makes our lives complete and satisfied. But if that happiness goes against the natural laws that God created, you will never find true happiness, and you must change your set ways.

No one ever says I want to come in second place, so strive to be victorious in all your dealings.

If you give a greedy man an inch, he will take a yard; if you give him a yard, he will take the whole field; but if you give them what he deserves in the first place, which is nothing, he will beg for an inch and be satisfied with whatever he can get his hands onto.

What's mine is now yours, and what yours is now mine, but what's God's is everything the both of you have.

If there's a disagreement among the people, a king should have the wisdom to judge them fairly.

The non-believer steals faith, hope, and love from the faithful through his vain and unrighteous actions. Don't fall victim to their nonsense and ignorance; they know no better and have never experienced the true meaning of gentle love. Pray for them and their salvation.

Having beef with someone is like having water stuck in your ear.

You can't knock it out, and it only causes infection.

Don't get spiritual advice from someone who doesn't believe in Jesus Christ. It's like pounding your fist against the wall on purpose.

There are several ways to make love to a woman without having sexual contact. One is writing poetry for them. Another way is to write a song for them. Another way is to listen to their every frustration and try to fix it. Another way is to paint a portrait of them. Another way is to constantly compliment them on their beautiful ways. These are just a couple of examples, but there are many ways to make love without falling victim to your lustful desires.

Trial and error are the names of the learning game. How many times you play determines the amount of success you will have later in life.

Don't bring a knife to a gunfight, and don't bring a gun to a knife fight. But just put the knife and the gun down, to begin with, before someone really gets hurt and avoid the fight altogether.

A lion doesn't take crap from anyone. That's the spirit of a winner.

Watching porn can be considered cheating on a lover whose heart is true.

Take off the chemical makeup and wake up before your sleep shortens and your dreams disappear.

Having a strong will and drive is necessary when accomplishing the impossible.

Having some faith can get you to heaven's gates, but having super faith will get you through with no problems.

Hug life.

Your destiny was determined before you were born. You're exactly who you are supposed to be, so don't worry about where you are in life. You're in the right place right now.

Richard Wislocky

You must be in it to win it. So, when you join, come with a winning attitude.

A spiritual hammer can bring a thunderous bang from miles away.

If you're having trouble with the connection, pray harder.

True love has no time for disappointments. It delivers.

True love has no doubt but is based on super faith.

By faith, God will answer your prayers.

Through hope, a lover can dream again.

With love, God works the impossible.

By faith, we trust in the heart of a lover.

Hope is found through determination.

Love can change the outcome to righteousness.

Faith must be sustained with great vision.

Hope tells a failure to try again.

Love brings happiness.

Faith is forged from a skinny pathway.

Hope can be felt at the dawn of enlightenment.

Understanding breeds love.

Faith is never blind.

Hope can ease a heavy decision.

Love is spawned when two souls surrender to one another.

Faith is not a hot house establishment.

Hope can be found in a dream with family.

Love seeks to be fertile.

Faith is a pregnant woman.

Hope comes from nurturing devotion.

Love makes evil dissipate.

Faith flies through a cloudy storm.

Proverbs

Hope is the birth of a baby elephant.
Love is when that baby elephant stands.
Faith is believing in God's goodness.
Hope carries sorrow to distant lands.
Love is the heat from a peacock's egg.
Faith can make a small man tall.
Hope brings will to troubled hearts.
Lovers are seen kissing on top of the Empire State Building.
Faith comes when romance is nurtured.
Hope can be found singing in unison.
Love is romantic when two hearts moan.
Faith is built through prayers to your Father.
Hope is a light creeping through the darkness.
Love keeps you young and ageless in your heart.
Faith makes itself known through the birth of wisdom.
Hope can never be killed.
Love is the planning of an unborn child.
Faith takes control where doubt once lived.
Hope finds those with tons of great vision.
Love can change the air in a smokey room.
Faith is kind to those who seek.
Hope makes a prayer fly.
Love is how we change the world.
Faith comes from a place of truth.
Hope brings out the best-case scenario.
Love is making your lover smile.
Faith comes with a peace of mind.
Hope is retained by those with desires.
Love needs no introduction.
Faith is having trust in your steps.

Hope is built upon the wantonness of fools.
Love can see through the darkness.
Faith is the birthplace of wisdom.
Hope can alter a careless accident.
Love breaks through any wall.
Faith comes from the love of our Father.
Hope is needed when a mob is rebuking.
Love plants the seeds of our future.
Faith can be heard in the halls of churches.
Hope is a basket of offerings.
Love must be seen in the faces of strangers.
Faith is a homeless man begging.
Hope is found in the prayers of a child.
Love needs two to bring it alive.
Faith comes from many breakthroughs.
Hope is generated by wishful thinking.
Love is gentle.
Faith is seen in the acts of believers.
Hope makes terror not prosper.
Love comes from an abominably will.
Faith is the message of Jesus.
Hope can be seen in the works of Jesus.
Love is what God gives the world.
Faith makes disciples.
Hope is in a mother's worries.
Love is calling the wicked.
Faith jumps over the fire.
Hope makes lovers go searching.
Love is found in the water.
Faith melts through any ice block.

Hope keeps dreamers searching.
Love is a turtle's strong heart.
Faith will always be waiting.
Hope must breathe where there's darkness.
Love can climb any mountain.
Faith is felt through the darkness.
Hope carries no burden.
Love eats with a family.
Faith should never go backward.
Hope is constantly pending.
Love greets with soft kisses.
Faith is the love of our Father.
Hope is our Father's wishes.
Love comes from our Father.
Faith greets with salvation.
Hope kills all the doubt.
Love is the greatest.
Faith is built by pushing backward.
Hope can sing in a war zone.
Love is an "Amen."
Loyalty is for the faithful.
Hopelessness doesn't exist.
Love needs tender affection.
Faith is a staircase we climb unconsciously.
Hope is carried by the true believers.
Love changes but remains the same.
Faith is seen by the eyes of the searching.
Hope is given when seeking a resolution.
Love endures through thick and thin.
Faith can never be unworthy.

Hope is needed for those who suffer.
Love comes naturally when it's surrounded by sweetness.
Faith is calmness in a mob of noisy strangers.
Hope is sung in freedom songs.
Love is needed twenty-four hours a day, seven days a week.
Baptism is holy with water.
Never come between a man and his family.

When you're pushing the limits of what is known to be correct, don't be shocked when it blows up in your face, for when you take a risk, you risk being taken care of.

True love will always be there, ready to catch and nurture you with kindness and sweetness and understanding if needed.

There is a burning and eternal flame that exists between lovers; it burns when two hearts act as one.

Wisdom can be obtained by a series of unfortunate events.

A dog's bark or snarl will always alert you of something, so pay attention to those who have ears.

Say you don't want or don't wish to, but never say that you can't or that it's not possible.

If it's sin, and what they do is inhuman, I don't think you want to play a game that you'll think you'll never win.

Holy Communion is about the forgiveness of sins through the taking of the Holy Sacraments, the blood and body of Christ.

Don't be so serious that you forget how to laugh and have a good time.

Most sins are not by chance but deliberate.

The words of the grandfather speak through his grandchildren, and they have a special connection.

Nobody likes a winning child. Stop this behavior before it becomes out of control, or else he will rain terror on the entire family.

There is nothing more gratifying and rewarding than hearing a child pray.

Someone who is always tardy was never taught the value of time and being on time. It is just disrespectful to always be late.

The answers to a child's homework are more important than you think.

It is better to be sharp than to be cloudy and confused.

Use only the bare minimum, and try not to be wasteful or live in excess.

Don't make accusations unless you know 100 percent that that's the way it went down. Do not falsely accuse someone or ruin their reputation on purpose.

Take care of business swiftly. Nip things in the bud. Do not let things lag on and on.

Do not take bedding with a cruel and unjust woman; this will only bring you sorrow.

Blocking someone and then unblocking them is like having your teeth pulled slowly, one by one. You blocked them for a reason in the first place. Always remember that before you go crawling back and lower your standards.

You don't ever want to be accused of not playing with a full deck of cards.

There's no such thing as shaming the person you love.

Sometimes, there must be consequences for your actions. Without consequence, there would be no law. With no law, there wouldn't be civilization as we know it.

Sometimes, we must make sacrifices; without sacrifice, there shall be no reward.

Sometimes in life, we must do things that we normally wouldn't do. That we never choose to.

The truth will set you free, but free from what is the question?

People don't have to know everything you always do. There are some things you must leave private, or else they will hold you accountable for every little thing you do. Privacy is the key to a healthy self-reflection.

When objects in the mirror are closer than what they are, it's best to take caution of all your surroundings.

People weren't built to withstand more than a few minutes of being on the wire. Life on it will only consume your every thought and emotion until you are left with just a raw essence of what life should have been before you came into judgment.

People need something to believe in; whether it's good or bad, they always will want to believe in something. Show and prove to them the truth, and they will follow.

After you are done looking around for love, just become it, and love will find you sooner or later.

If you can't take it easy on yourself, how do you expect others to treat you?

We are not supposed to judge others; we are all sinners, and that is an honest judgment.

All the sickness chatter ruins any sort of self-worth, and it is not needed.

Don't bring out the hate parade because it seems to last forever sometimes. One hate leads to another. Just bring love to the love parade.

When you set your sights on negative talks, negative things will happen. Don't mention the foul stuff from the beginning, and you should not fall victim to it. Hold your words with goodness and be kind-natured from the start.

It takes the power of a gentle yet strict love to make a serious change.

You can fortify and strengthen the armor of God that He gives you to fight with through faith.

Whatever there is a question to, there lays an answer too.

It is impossible to kiss correctly if you're grinding your teeth.

There shall be no shame felt when you're in God's favor.

Be grateful for what you have because it could always be a lot worse than what it is.

Even when we think we have it all figured out, there's always the next lesson to be learned.

Love remains the same, but it can change in the drop of a heartbeat.

A quiet night can easily be ruined by the voice of a stranger.

Just bringing love takes years of suffering.

Whatever is holding you back from your full blessings must be let go of before it consumes your every thought and want. You know what the problem is, too, but most of the time, you are just in denial and lying to yourself.

It takes twisted emotions and a burning passion to bring forth the greatness of spirit.

It's possible to become a gentle rage. This, too, must be corrected.

No matter how empty your heart becomes, it is always making more room for fullness of love, and that is what it seeks in the end.

Have the pallet for great colors to shine.

"Chocolate Rain" is a song sung with hope.

Rock beats scissors and a piece of paper.

Every Which Way but Loose is not just a movie but a mind state.

Revenge is an ice-cold dish, and there are excellent waiters.

Comparing one's love to sunshine is a great honor.

The only rule love has is to love.
Love has many teachers.
Love is the fans who sit in the bleachers.
Love is a bunch of pandas sliding down a slide.
Love coming calling, for it we shall abide.
Love puts together the missing pieces to life's puzzle.
Love is determination, might, and hustle.
Love is a polar bear with her cubs playing in the snow.
Love plants seeds and watch's them grow.
Love happens when two souls melt together.
Love is the four seasons and all of the vast weather.
Love is like an exotic rare spice.
Love shall always suffice.
Love can be cruel if one person lies.
Love is in the mighty eagle's eyes.
Love is found in the pages of the Bible.
Love is the drum hitting so tribal.
Love is seen in the eyes of an elder.
Love is the shield that protects the wielder.
Love brings a warm fuzzy feeling.
Love for prayers when we are kneeling.
Love gives hate a gentle beat down.
Love can always reverse a frown.
"Love one another" is God's word.
Love for the preacher that you heard.
Love for the Tri-Lambs and the Nerds.
Love for the antelope running in herds.
Love for the horses eating Reggie Bars.
Love for the man who is going to be sinning on Mars.
Love for Philippe Petit and his cloud dance.

Proverbs

Love for the millions of tiny red ants.
Love for Joseph when his brothers sold him.
Love for the health nuts pumping in the gym.
Love for Rahab; she was a harlot.
Love for the color crimson scarlet.
Love for the Count when he counts.
One… two… three… four… love counts.
Love for Ruth at the feet of her man.
Love for Boaz, who had a master grand plan.
Love for Esther and her new king.
Love is seeing what good love brings.
Joy can be mass-produced by the doing of good deeds.
Joy is watching the full growth of planted seeds.
Joy is the birth of two lover's child.
Joy is a stranger passing by who went and smiled.
Joy, when expressed, is triumphant and sound.
Joy is the fires that blaze in the campgrounds.
.

Joy is the "J" in the abbreviation "7J."
Joy means "Jesus" in the abbreviation "7J."
Joy can be harvested in the path of righteousness.
Joy is walking the path of righteousness.
Joy is something that is pleasant and soothing by nature.
Joy is something loving and mature.
Joy is the exclamation of something holy and grand.
Joy is the sand dripping through your toes as you walk through the sand.
Joy is a book written by Bishop Tutu and the Dalai Lama.
Joy is when there is no baby mama drama.
Joy is the different color of lights every night on the Empire

State Building.

Joy is the accomplishment of building the Empire State Building.

Joy is a basket of fresh fruits and cheeses.
Joy is the bread and body broken off by Jesus.
Joy is when the home team wins.
Joy is when we give up sins.
Joy is a lover waiting for her love.
Joy is the mourn of a mourning dove.
Joy can bring any frown upside down.
Joy is the end-all purpose of clowns.
Joy is manifested in the presence of elephants.
Joy is found in a sanctuary of elephants.
Joy is a dolphin doing lots of flips.
Joy is when a goal is scored from massive soccer kicks.
Joy stays tight with those of kind heart.
Joy is the effort to make sacred art.
Joy brings love anytime it's around.
Joy will turn any frown upside down.
Joy is the grace we say before every meal.
Joy is a good reputation and mass appeal.
Joy leaves smiles on discolored faces.
Joy is the bonding of many different races.
Joy is a toy for the wise and worthy.
Joy is making a wish at 11:11 and 11:30.
Joy can hold a symbolic nature.
Joy is not for all of the haters.
Joy is knowing the truth in a situation.
Joy is not becoming a victim of masturbation.
Joy can be felt in the hearts of the wild.

Joy is rocking a newborn child.
Joy makes pain do the spits.
Joy is where freedom sits.
Joy can be sustained in the presence of the worthy.
Joy would never go and hurt me.
Joy for my lady when she holds me down.
Joy for the roller coaster going upside down.
Joy for Moses when he parted the sea.
Joy is a gift for you and me.
Joy is an ice-cream truck coming down the block.
Joy is for the Eagle that sits upon the Eagle Rock.
Stay on a narrow path, for that is the one that leads to heaven.

Spiritually evolve, and you will become a preacher of the word yourself. It's only evolution.

When you ask God a question, wait for His answer before rushing to action.

Give help to those in need and always be willing to go the extra mile.

"God did not create poverty; we did by our inability to share" (Mother Teresa).

A rich king and a man in poverty have more in common than you think. They both have the breath of life that God gave them.

The Lord will giveth, and the Lord will taketh if that's what pleases Him.

If you always give in to when a child moans and complains, they will never learn self-control.

After you have set your boundaries with a woman, do not fall back into temptation, or else your problem will get even worse than before you originally set those boundaries.

In the art of war, never underestimate your enemy's agenda. Be wary of random kind gestures of affection, for they cloak and hide the real message, which is usually more war and betrayal.

A scammer will stop at nothing until they feel they are satisfied and paid in some fashion. Especially if you can never find out who they really are or where they are really scamming you from. Just like you, they have a blanket of securities ready for your every move if you counterplay them or try to stop them. Praying for a peaceful solution is your only solution.

Sometimes, a prayer is all we have, so pray and hope that God answers.

Performing random acts of kindness goes a long way on the spiritual karma meter.

Just do your best; that's all we can really hope for. A full effort has its blessings.

Sometimes, our ego can hinder the outcome of a solution, and sometimes, it can get us through the doorways faster. Our ego has a very strong influence over our actions. Keep it in check.

Try not to be indebted to anyone financially. Living below the negative line can be trying on the soul.

Whether you're rich or poor, always try to come correct in your payments and balances.

This is very important to learn right away: don't spend what you don't have.

Credit cards are no different than loan sharks; they both are designed to keep you paying, and they both have the ability to break your soul and spirit.

If you abuse a lover's love, you can't expect them to just come waltzing back into your life again as strongly as they did before you hurt them; even if forgiveness is there, respect and trust are still missing, which will always hold them back from completely loving

Proverbs

you properly again.

You can't always do what everybody wants you to do. At some point, you must think for yourself and make your own decisions in order to grow properly.

Never make close friends with another man's wife; it will always put doubt in his mind about their own relationship.

You should always meet the demand of a friend's request, even if you don't want to. He wouldn't be asking if he didn't need something. Do unto others as you'd do to yourself.

Sometimes, having no money will slow a party down, but it will enlighten your soul in some fashion.

Giving someone the silent treatment is a major sign of disrespect. And you'll never solve a problem with the silent treatment; it's always too painful to do any good.

When destiny comes calling, make sure you drop what you're doing and pick up the phone for it.

A foolish man will always have an excuse for his poor actions. A wise man will always have responsibility for his own actions.

Sometimes, you must make your presence scarce in order to be taken seriously when you do arrive. Sometimes, saying less can be more too.

Never quit on a friend because you're scared of what he means for the changing of you. Be loyal through thick and thin, and you shall never fall.

"Real freedom is having nothing. I was freer when I didn't have a cent" (Mike Tyson).

Kissing can be one of the most sacred things we can do on earth. Be grateful for those who get to do this activity, and affection of love, for it can change a person's world for the better and influence a nation if witnessed.

Nothing can ever become good or be good when you have to crawl through a window.

When you start to forget the simplest of memories, you know it's time to fold and start praying.

Living in the world makes worldly things happen. Living for the church makes spiritual things happen.

Keep a sober mind about things, and never walk through your days drunk.

Sins may cause you temporary blindness.

After many sorrows and trials comes a great blessing; seize it and don't fall backward.

God knows what you need all the time, so don't worry about it because He's already on your case, trying to make you better and stronger. Recognize the signs and make corrections when it's presented.

Keep your tongue braided; you'll live longer and have fewer conflicts of interest with the world's challenges.

Love is like a Snoopy snow cone on a hot summer day.

Love is the flowers that bloom in May.

Love is a fire hydrant shooting water out for tons of kids to play in and cool off from the summer heat.

Love is the greatest; it can't be beat.

When faith grabs your attention, hang on for dear life.

Hope is planted with every good deed we sow and is in all seeds that grow.

Love is a show tune sung from a Broadway show.

The greater the love, the greater God's test will be to test it.

The greater the love, the greater God will bless it.

Once you have survived a burning ring of fire, you can survive just about anything in any condition.

Never raise your voice at someone, even if they're your lover. A raised voice is a sign of weakness and is disrespectful and just plain hostile.

Giving your time and energy to help a food bank or homeless shelter is a labor of love.

Become a good helper and someone who people can count on when help is needed. This is a good thing.

Teachers teach you things you did not understand or know of, they also are responsible for delivering the word.

A church gives oneself a sense of belonging. With belonging comes comfort and community and self-worth.

Are you looking for inspiration? Go to church, and you shall find it there.

Being sad and lonely and depressed should never be an issue if you're living for God's mission.

You can conquer any task at hand with the help of prayer and God's love.

You should never feel unworthy or unwanted for being in God's path. You are more precious than all the gold and silver in the world, and you are always needed for some great spiritual task somewhere at some time.

Whenever you go to someone's house, try and bring a little housewarming gift as a token of appreciation for their hospitality.

The tired man gets nothing done but sleep; if only the world could come to his bedside, he could be a success. You must force yourself to get up, get out, and get something.

Chasing women around for lustful adventures is like an elephant getting his foot stuck in a tire swing.

You can have all the wartime prayers in the world to fight off a legion of demons, but if the fire in your eye is out, they are all useless.

Watch what you say, for even your words hold weight on the scales of justice.

Always be grateful; even when something bad happens, you must be grateful.

Bickering about who said this or who said that is pointless in the grand scheme of things. Try not to bicker or argue.

Love is someone carrying water in a jug on their head, walking back from the well barefooted.

Albino eagles kill the snakes of shame.

Wisdom is a level of consciousness that can only be obtained from a series of unfortunate events.

A lot of humans live like vultures; they circle and scavenge around delis, looking for the fresh pieces of dead meat that someone else has killed for them.

I don't believe in being a vegan enthusiast, but it has its rewards.

Everybody likes a good tragedy; that is why we watch so much TV.

Giving birth to a child is one of the greatest blessings one can ever receive from God.

All evil fades to dust in the arms of a lover.

One thing that life has taught us is that there is someone for everyone. Keep searching, and you will find them. God will bring you the right one eventually. Have faith.

Will you be ready when they sound the horns and the stars fall? Repent and get right now, for when the end of days comes, it shall come like a thief in the night.

The Blood Moon is not a myth, and it will come someday to wreak havoc on the earth in the end of days.

The message of seven great horned owls hooting is that "we're cutting down all the trees, and they have no place to go anymore."

There are four horses that are ready to ride, and then there'll be nowhere to hide.

Many will claim to be Jesus in the last days, but there is only one Jesus Christ.

Joy and pain, sunshine and rain.

You can never beat King Solomon unless you're a lily in the field.

GOoD.

When you cross one line, it leads to another and then another after that.

The spirit police and the shame police have the same objective every once in a while. Try to avoid both from correcting you.

Don't make promises you can't keep.

When you are led into temptation, just lead yourself right back out; avoid the mistakes.

When you're sorry, you're sorry, and sometimes a sorry person has to pay for his mistakes.

When someone knows your every move at every second of the day, it can't be good even if you have the best of intentions; there should always be some mystery left in the one you love. A little mystery is healthy for a relationship.

Never be too far gone that you can't make it back with a little repentance from a couple of prayers. If a prayer won't help you, you definitely went too far.

We are humans filled with desires and needs, and if they're not met by a significant other, then one might look elsewhere. But if all your wants and needs are met and you look elsewhere, you are just selfish, and you deserve what you have coming to you.

How can you truly be sorry if there are no consequences?

Sometimes, you wish you could turn back time. And sometimes, time turns its back on you.

People say, "I'll sleep when I'm dead." This is a horrible phrase because you need your dreams and your proper sleep, or else you turn into a monster, and you become the living dead.

It is better to say nothing and have no negative thoughts in your area than to poison a good thing with something negative, no matter how big or small it is. It always brings out the negative.

Be careful what you do to someone you love or once loved because a little birdy might just go and whisper it into their ear and ruin everything for you if you're not careful or truthful.

Silence is more precious than a high-speed train going from London to Paris. Praise God for giving you silence.

After two many years of being tortured, there's only one thing to do, and that is to breathe love.

When you're in love, every breath is spent on your significant other. Just don't forget that the breath of life was the first gift God gave to you before you were in love.

Live a life free from saying "I'm sorry" and free from saying "Forgive me."

The life of a sinner seems to fade when you've found true love. All your problems seem to disappear, and you are planted on a good, narrow path.

Never be too timid to tell a stranger, "I love you" or "God bless you."

If a lot of people tend to disagree with the truth you display, then that's a good thing, and you know you're on the right path. The truth was made for everyone, but many find it so hard to accept, and they take out their frustration on you for telling it how it is when they're dead wrong.

A best friend will tell you how it is, and he is honored for this, but only you know what's right and wrong for you. Listen to your heart first, even if it's wrong. You must follow your own heart, or else you will never grow into the person you want to be. Sure, there'll be many mistakes.

To have more than five dreams a night is a blessing if you can remember them all. But just remember there's always one in there to throw you off from your own spiritual direction and does not have your best interests. Learn to recognize the tares and rebuke them from their roots.

Drugs will kill your dream life. Cut them out and watch as your dreams flourish once again.

Drug dreams are never good, even if you're getting high on them, because they will always keep you in a state of temptation, and this is not spiritual but antispiritual. Lead us not into temptation.

Never cheat on a lover; you are just cheating yourself out of something that could have been good.

When you live for true love, your heart now beats for two, and you have twice the responsibly to behold now. If you can't handle the pressure, don't get involved in the first place.

Listen to the voice that tells you you're wrong, it may be the only truth that someone's going to share with you. Consider it a blessing to be corrected from it.

Proverb: a short and pithy saying in general use, stating a gentry truth or a piece of advice.

Define your reasons behind something, and you will have your just cause.

When your stomach moans, it needs something to eat. When your heart moans, it needs someone to love you.

You will never get or obtain your full blessings if you keep half-assing it. Go the distance.

Be a part of the solution and not the problem.

Every cheater will have his day like every rose has a thorn.

You yourself are the best at what you do and who you are. Therefore, you deserve the best of everything. You are worthy.

Forgiveness is an extremely hard thing to do if it's not in your heart to do it.

Forgiveness allows mending, and I'll hold you right to it.

Forgiveness is still mighty, even for a lurch.

Forgiveness can manifest from the lessons and scriptures you learn in church.

Forgiveness is about letting go of the past and letting it be for what it is.

Forgiveness can rekindle your faith and all of your rizz.

Forgiveness is a good tool to build your future on.

Forgiveness is a flock of doves that put you on.

Forgiveness is gained through the fellowship of the church.

Forgiveness sometimes manifests when we go to church.

Forgiveness is for the strong and not the weak.

Forgiveness should be sustained seven days a week.

Forgiveness can make the scorner to seek.

Forgiveness is bold and never bleak.

Draw the circle wide. No one stands alone; we stand side by side. Draw the circle wide.

It is God who delivers time and time again.

"Blessed is he whose transgression is forgiven, whose sin is covered. Blessed is the man unto whom the Lord imputeth not iniquity, and in whose spirit there is no guile" (Psalm 32:1–2).

In order to be the change you want to be in this world, you must first manifest it with your mouth and words to bring it forth.

Proverbs

A wise man once said never to date a woman who has a foul mouth; her actions will follow.

It is foolish to ponder if you can change the world, but it is wise to believe that you can do it.

Never make a king wait unless it's a prophecy; that takes time for God to answer.

Flattery will get you anywhere you want, but wise men know better.

Keep the love with every step you take. Love will put a pep in your step.

Soulmates do exist, and we get a chance to be with them in just about every lifetime we spend on the earth.

There is a club where the sun doesn't shine; they steal your love, soul, body, and mind.

It takes twenty dollars to play a game you cannot win; being born a mortal is your only sin.

Crack babies come into the world fighting addiction. What sort of righteous path is this? Pretty heavy stuff for a newborn to deal with. Don't smoke crack or do drugs while you're pregnant, please.

In some places in the world, you can't get a clean drop of water to drink that isn't corroded or contaminated. Praise the Lord for the clean water that you drink.

When you're knocking on heaven's door, you better hope that they can hear you.

Justice and joy go hand in hand.

Love is smelling the scent left behind on your lover's pillow.

A king must have a direct connection to the Lord in order to stay righteous at all times.

Anytime you feel you need to make a connection with a deceased loved one, you can try and ask for them to help you, and they will come down to comfort you in your times of trouble somehow. You must look for the connections; they will be there for you. One of a soul's jobs in the afterlife is to help those who are in need back on earth. So, yes, it is possible. Joy.

You can conquer any feat through the power of love.

Praying together goes further than the prayers of just one.

Lovers can stop time.

The act of holding hands is a very powerful sign of affection and should be done more often.

Two people in love in faith can move twice as many mountains.

Grace's cousin is forgiveness.

When something is done with grace, it is usually flawless and serene.

A light touch from a loved one can be healing in so many ways.

Angels of light have the ability to work on hearts and give renewal to all areas of the sickness in the body.

When lovers intwine, guardian angels dance in their honor.

Negativity cannot penetrate where love blossoms.

It is always good to have an emergency plan for loved ones if disaster strikes so that everybody can find each other. Take the time to plan ahead, even for the smallest of catastrophes.

God made the ocean so it cannot be measured in depth, so it can be said for true love.

To teach a hater to love, you must show them a love that they didn't know existed.

God's love has been proven to be the dominating force on earth; those who think otherwise just are inexperienced.

Bad things happen to good people because there is a higher purpose, and they have the ability to endure it, whatever it may be.

Sweetness and goodness walk hand in hand.

Proverbs

You better find a place to hide when bulls are on parade.

There is no shame in having two different sizes of shoes. As long as they fit, wear it.

Man can never measure an earthquake's size.

Even thunder and lightning have an order.

You better be prepared in case a tree falls on your house.

True love is like a runaway train that never falls off the tracks.

You can alter history just by saying, "I love you."

It doesn't matter whether you win or lose; what matters is whether you have God on your side or not.

Soon, there will be a man sinning on Mars.

You can't break what has already been broken; you can only mend it.

If your words don't inspire, then they shouldn't be said.

Wisdom can be found in the beeps of an ER ward.

If yawning is contagious, then so can loving be.

There is a message to be found in everything that exists.

Wisdom shines when proverbs come alive.

Good love is like a well-greased oiled machine.

One greedy act leads to another and another.

You cannot stop the dealings of rocks.

The expression "having a heart of gold" can be both a blessing and a curse.

You want to big-up someone and never belittle them.

Bad things happen to people whose behavior is "apushious."

You cannot rewrite or change God's law; it's the law.

It's better to be known as a wise man than a wise guy.

Keeping it real can never go wrong as long as the truth is behind it.

Constructive criticism is wanted, but deconstructive insults are not.

If I had a penny for my thoughts, I'd be a millionaire, but then I wouldn't be thinking.

Fighting with your best friend is like killing your soul; don't do it.

Don't put off till tomorrow what you can do today.

Jealousy will make one do just about the stupidest of things. Leave this emotion to wither away on its own. Don't react. Time can and will heal you.

Have some sort of creative outlet to channel your feelings out into the world. Don't bottle them all up inside because you'll tend to lose them because there are so many. Have an external emotional output.

Cameras and photographs capture a piece of a person's soul when a photo is taken.

When an animal speaks, you better listen.

Bury Heart :: Wounded Knee

Tears of a Clown :: Ears of Corn

Tiny Bear :: Fish dance

Little Turtle :: Big Bird

Ghost Dog :: Blind Spirit

Sweet Heart :: Water Drink

Camp Fire :: Broad Way

Schools Cool :: Mega Fish

Proverb :: Wisdom

Wise :: Watchful

Feeling Good :: Smoking Rocks

Green Witch :: Gentle Giant

Square :: Circle

GOoD Ness :: Sweet Ness

Proverbs

2 Blue :: Eagle Stick
Oak Tree :: Eagle Rock
911 :: Angels in Heaven
Dance Hall :: Fluffy Pounce
Warning Sign :: Blood Moon
Big Blue :: Seahorse Legs
Stealth Bomber :: Dream Maker
Many Names :: Many Voices
Gentle Rain :: Crying Dove
Jews :: Christians
Holy Ghost :: Hard Worker
Peace Tank :: Rain Maker
Doggie Paddle :: Sloths Swimming
Ruth :: Ester
Enoch :: Metatron
Butterflies :: Dancing
UU :: VV
Sleepy Tiger :: New York City
Sleeping Chief :: Navajo Princess
Sacred Book :: Many Authors
Windy Forest :: Tree Ghost
Windy Church :: Falling Tree
Mustard Seed :: Spiritual Salad
I had a Dream :: We had a Dream
Martin Luther King Jr. :: Mahatma Gandhi
Mother Teresa :: Eagle Spirit
Tired Preacher :: Dusty Sandel's
Gentle Snow :: Mourning Dove
Vulture Feeding :: Deli Meats
Gentle Women :: Eagle Rocking

True Colors :: Soul Mates

Cranberries :: Strawberries

Indian Road :: Jesus Walking

Inyan Cante :: Sacred Blessing

Turtle's Love :: Turtle's Heart

House Music :: Angel Singing

Buffalo Hide :: Birds Nest

Bi Polar Bear :: Brink of Destruction

Pure Nirvana :: Peacocks Egg

White Lights :: Elephant Baby

Hood River :: Drinking Water

Ellora Caves :: Blue Elephants

Mayan Priest :: Naked Jesus

Heavens Door :: Holy Organ

Flying Angel :: White Dragon

Holy Nations :: Raining Desert

Best Friend :: GOoD Partner

Sun Drops :: Stars Falling

Rock :: Hope

Sometimes, it's best to let your partner take the lead.

No more suffering on earth; that is, once again, the final goal.

"Excellence is being able to perform at a high level over and over again. You can hit a half-court shot once. That's just the luck of the draw. If you consistently do it…that's excellence" (Jay-Z).

When telling the truth gets you in trouble, don't feel ashamed; you did the right thing.

When love grows cold, you best have something to warm you up.

When all your wisdom fails, you weren't that wise.

It is love when someone shares your reflections.

Don't disrespect the gifts; they were given with affection and love.

To have a ride or die is considered a blessing.

For one to obtain true love, there must be sacrifice.

Only a fool would choose a material object over the love that comes from one's heart.

Making love is one of the greatest paintings you can ever make.

Avoid using the crying face emoji.

There is nothing like the uplifting spirit of a sunny snow day.

The poems of a lover can engrave a voice of happiness in the heart and soul for seasons to come.

When you're too eager, that's when your judgment gets cloudy.

All of your greatest joys become all of your greatest pains.

Never wake a sleeping lion.

Sometimes, your presence is needed. Be present at that time.

There is a time to push and a time to pull.

Greater things happen when you remain loyal to your lover.

It's not fair to do something when someone else who's close to you can't.

It's always good to have a friend that will take the fears away in times of trouble.

Sometimes, we just take the wrong path, and we must backtrack to the right one.

Carrying guilt and shame around can be a sickness; you must let it go like a bad habit before it consumes you.

Sometimes, you have to take the long way home.

It is selfish to lay negative thoughts in a group that is having fun and enjoying themselves.

Always be prepared to go the extra mile if necessary. You have to always be ready for uncertainty.

Talking too much can sometimes ruin the atmosphere.

Go out of your way to help those who help you.

One must have patience when waiting for something rewarding.

True love can never be altered even if you're having a bad day; it only supports you.

Loyalty is precious, like finding two pearls in an oyster.

What you think is wrong is wrong, and nobody can change that.

Count thy blessings and be grateful for what you have.

When someone gives you bad advice, just say thank you and brush it off; don't take time to correct them; they will only see it as an insult, but in some cases, correction is needed.

One man's trash is another man's treasure.

When every love song you hear in the world applies to you and your lover, you know you're in love.

To become a preacher is an honor. Everyone should strive to become one, for this is what God wants for us. Evolve.

Doing an act of creativity together with someone or many others holds twice as many blessings.

Negative influences shall not be tolerated when positivity is shining.

All that was, all that is, and all that is to be is embedded in the river of scars deep within.

Green and white lights are healing colors.

To be in the cave or to be out of the cave? That is the question. How about both at the same time?

It is possible to be in two different locations at the same time.

I think I can; I think I can; I think I can. I must; I must; I must.

Rising to the occasion can sometimes be lying down to rest and breathe.

Terrors await you if you live your life terrified, but only joys await you when you free your love.

Feel-good stories should be more prevalent in the News, for there is far too much tragedy in broadcasting.

Do not be standing backward at the front of the line.

Nothing is more joyfully tasty than eating a fresh icicle or some fresh powder snowball.

True love breaths with every breath you take.

To be honest and fair are two good qualities to have.

Sometimes, less says more.

You can never have too much "I love you."

Love is a whale that jumps and swims.

Love is a coffee filled to the brim.

Love is when God forgives our sin.

Love is when the home team wins.

Love for you and your next of kin.

Love for many colors of skin.

Love for the people who are Mexican.

Love is thick and never thin.

Love on a cold day with a shot of gin.

Love is peaceful and never grim.

Love for the yang and the yin.

Love for the Grand Canyon, standing on the brim.

Love is a haircut with a good trim.

Love is a dunk slammed in the rim.

Love for the tiny boy named Tim.

Love always shines and is never dim.

Love gives and never takes.

Love is too real, not for the fakes.

Love for Jesus and for His sake.

Love is the cookies that a mother bakes.

Richard Wislocky

No love for phonies, frauds, or fakes.
But love for the phonies, frauds, and fakes.
Love is the records held in the crates.
Love is creating and what art makes.
Love for the bakery and all of its cakes.
Love is forgiving; that is what it takes.
Love is a seed, and watching it grow.
Love is the main event at the show.
Love is "yo" responded with "yo."
Love for the dog walking yo-yo.
Love is being clean from head to toe.
Love for the friend and for the foe.
Love's a green light; steady you go.
Love is a boat ride in which you must row.
Love for the words in the poem that you woo.
Love says yes, while hate says no.
Love is the seeds that we sow.
Love is the greatest, and now you know.
Love for Hamas and the Jews.
Love is a preacher with the good news.
Love can always chase away the blues.
With love, you can never lose.
Love for the fisherman chasing clues.
Love for the W and the UU's.
Love is a kiss on a bruise.
Love has respect; it pays its dues.
Love for the cow that goes moo.
Love for the animals in every zoo.
Love is something to always choose.
Love can be found in church pews.

Proverbs

Love is contagious; watch it ooze.
Love from New Year's ball drop kazoos.
Love is the power that we must use.
Love is when we carry Grandpa's canoe.
Love had King David for his eight wives.
Love can never cut like a knife.
Love is a tasty, spicy green chive.
Love is always taken in stride.
Love Angelou and all of her My's.
Love for the baby when it cries.
Love for the second and third tries.
Love for a lover on a late-night drive.
Love is the cure, the bandage and ties.
Love in the mirror when looking in the eyes.
Love forgives all for all of the lies.
Love is something you can never buy.
Love for grandpa and grandma.
Love to sing Fa So La Di Da.
Love for a lover I call Mama.
Love is abundant; go get a lot.
Love for the ER when you get shot.
Love is a gumbo mixed in a pot.
Love is yes and never a not.
Love in the vineyard and all of the crops.
Love holds a will that can never be dropped.
Love for the flag standing on top.
Love for soda that goes pop.
Love for the Eagle and the Rock.
When we fight addiction, we fight ourselves.
Anything you can do, I can do too. This should be the attitude.

Some paths we must walk alone, and some paths we must walk together.

Sometimes, all we need is a good shaking to set things straight.

Persistence is the key to success.

Love saves the day, each and every day.

Jesus saves.

Picture roots coming out of your feet with every step you take, and as they go into the ground, they expand and grow out to keep your balance grounded at all times. Then they suck back into your feet when you release the step. Whenever you're standing, have your roots expand deep into the ground so that you are firm and confident in your grounding at all times. This will help with your posture as well. Let the roots guide your steps to greatness.

Love will find a way; it always does.

There are many doors that get opened, and there are many doors that close; make sure you walk through the right ones at the right time. Timing is everything.

True love is sweet, like a strawberry field.

There's a gentle love in all our hearts, and God's got the key to unleash it.

No matter how many times you fall, you must try, try, try again.

Let love sustain your days and carry your nights.

Always remember that only a few are chosen.

If we looked for God just as hard as we look for someone to kiss, we would be putting a kiss before God's love, and His love is more important.

There's no need to argue anymore. Reach that level.

Have mercy for even the most corrupt of villains. He knows not what he does. Pray for them.

Whoever holds the microphone is your current preacher.

Faith, hope, and love can usually be found in a punk rock band.

"Madness in great ones must not unwatched go" (King Claudius).

Where there is music, there is expression, and this should not be overlooked.

If a picture says a thousand words, then a song says a million.

It is possible for bravery to be found when walking in depths of adversity.

Hope stays alive in the keepers of dreams.

It takes courage and prayers to bring a soul into this world.

If your window of opportunity is open, take it before you lose that blessing.

The impossible is possible; just ask Saint Jude.

You must have super faith when making a baby.

Recognize the correct signs that you're being attacked by the devil. He usually comes right before a great blessing to try and steal you away from it by leading you to sin. Be conscious of your actions at this time and steer clear of all evil and naughtiness.

When art manifests into real life is one of the greatest joys in the world.

True love will prevail through thick and thin, no matter the context or how hot the troubled waters are. True love is ruled by gentle love, and it conquers all.

Don't count your blessings before they hatch.

When God makes the stars or a star to align for you, you know you must be doing something powerful in the forces of love.

To make it rain in the valley of death is a great honor and brings faith, hope, love, and joy to the afflicted. It is a rare occasion and should be celebrated even though its face is shame.

True love shines more brightly than all the lights down in Times

Square together.

An eye for an eye never got anything but two eyes poked out.

The number seven is holy and can be found hundreds of times throughout the Bible.

True love can never part, no matter what the circumstance is or how badly someone wrongs the other. Forgiveness is always found.

True love will find a way through the darkness.

You cannot call yourself a healer if you say "F* God."

Religion is everywhere in everything.

Karma is an Indian ideal and is not considered to be a Christian concept.

The Blood Moon is real and will come to the earth one day to wreak havoc during the rapture.

> The greatest officially recorded number of children born to one mother is sixty-nine, to the wife of Feodor Vassilyev [her name was Valentina Vassilyev (1707–1782)], a peasant from Shuya, Russia. In twenty-seven confinements, she gave birth to sixteen pairs of twins, seven sets of triplets, and four sets of quadruplets.[3]

Green Life :: Urban Jungle

Open the flower :: Walk to shore

Hamas :: Jews

Big Pond :: Many Fish

42 Tribes :: Desert Rain

Sacred Symbols :: Reading Mirrors

3 :: 4

---

3 Guinness World Records, "Most prolific mother ever," accessed April 18, 2024, https://www.guinnessworldrecords.com/world-records/most-prolific-mother-ever.

Proverbs

34 :: 7

Hallelujah :: Enlightenment

Minds Melting :: Lights Chasing

Happy Trails :: Sacred Buttons

Joy Soaping :: Raining Lovers

Deer Beers :: Loving Spirits

Johnny Law :: Peace Treaty

Gods Grace :: Peaceful Race

Weeping Jesus :: Trail of Tears

Cuddles With Bears :: Facing Great Ness

Standing Bear :: Freedom Fighter

Kicking Bird :: Hidden Monsters

Sun Dance :: Sweet Heart

Rock Steady :: Break Dance

Tu-Pac :: Biggie Smalls

Big Snake :: Many Fight

Dee Brown :: Richard Erdoes

Sinful Nature :: Giant Serpent

Little Birds :: Saying Sorry

Thor :: Mariah

Blue MaCaw :: Feather God

Green Frog Skin :: Modern Day Slavery

Twin Gazelles :: Poetic Harmony

Wolves Dinner :: Black Sheep

Strange Woman :: Night Rider

Sun On :: Miami Melting

Heavy Sins :: Holy Preacher

Lo Ve :: Wash Tay

Proverbs :: Many Lessons

Another great thanks to God, Jesus, the Holy Ghost, and all the warm-hearted whispers that helped write this book along the way. All glory goes to God. Amen.

Milton Keynes UK
Ingram Content Group UK Ltd.
UKHW021447020924
447770UK00014B/824